MW01595811

At the **Foot**
C of the
ross

A 90-Day Devotional
for Becoming
Living Proof
of a **Loving God**
to a **Watching World**

by
Dwight Baker • Cindy Cañas
Mikelle Challenger • Patricia Dixon
Kim Lindquist • BJ Massa • Sharon Rigsby
Emily Ryan • Janie Southard
Donna Tovander

Copyright © 2011 by **Sagemont Church**
Dr. John D. Morgan, *Senior Pastor*
11300 South Sam Houston Parkway East, Houston, Texas 77089
www.sagemontchurch.org • 281.481.8770

ISBN 978-0-615-47116-7

Edited by
Linda Ausmus, Tammy Fort, Rosemary Rayburn,
Stuart Rothberg, Emily Ryan, and Jason Ryan

Cover Design by Marcos Medina
Book Design by Jason Ryan

Foreword

For many years millions of the followers of Jesus Christ have sung these words, "At the cross, at the cross, where I first saw the light and the burden of my heart rolled away." It is the desire of the writers of this practical life-changing series of devotionals to take you to the cross on which Jesus died for your sins and to inspire you with real life stories that mirror the challenges and opportunities you face every day. I encourage you to find a quiet place where you can get alone with God and take the time to prayerfully meditate on every thought. Once you are confident that you understand what the Holy Spirit has spoken into your heart, immediately look for ways to put the truth you have discovered into action and become Living Proof of a Loving God to a Watching World. We are praying that as you find yourself "at the foot of the cross," you will join us as we sing together, "It was there by faith I received my sight, and now I am happy all the day."

Dr. John D. Morgan
Senior Pastor, Sagemont Church

We'd love to hear about your own experience at the foot of the cross. Please email us at stories@sagemontchurch.org to share your story.

Table of Contents

1	Vertically Challenged	9
2	The Sweet Spot	13
3	He Knows My Voice	16
4	This Is My Story	19
5	We Okay, Daddy?	22
6	Failing to Forgive	25
7	Perfect Vision	28
8	Amber's Story	34
9	Men's Shoes… Size 10	37
10	What's That Smell?	40
11	You Said That Last Night!	44
12	Sharing Our Life Saver	47
13	White As Snow	50
14	Undignified	52
15	A Believing Heart	58
16	A Wedding and a Funeral	60
17	In Cinderella's Shadow	64
18	Freedom to Say His Name	68
19	The Dark Years	71
20	Angel in Grandmother's Clothing	74
21	God Loves a Fearful Giver?	78
22	Putting Feet to the Feat	83
23	Who's in Your Family Tree?	87
24	Why Not Me?	90
25	American Idols	93
26	Demolition Derby	96
27	Gagged and Dragged	99
28	The Blessings Book	103

29	Gardening of the Heart	108
30	Are You Under?	111
31	The Money Pit	114
32	There's No Place Like Home(s)	117
33	Be Strong and Take Heart	120
34	Too Much Weight?	122
35	Dig the Hole	124
36	My Will Be Done	130
37	Finding the Meaning of Mercy	133
38	Brownie Bottom Sundae	136
39	A Hug from Heaven	139
40	Life Begins at The Cross	142
41	God's Perfect Timing in an African Village	144
42	The Power of Water	147
43	The Rain Dance	152
44	It's the Real Thing	155
45	Got God?	157
46	Grape Jelly and Fruitfulness	159
47	The Still, Small Voice	162
48	Somebody May Be Watching You	165
49	Show Me a Sign	168
50	I Know Him!	173
51	It's All About Presentation	175
52	God's Instrument	179
53	Loving Hailey	182
54	Cast Your Cares Upon Him	186
55	Meeting Jesus, The Healer	189
56	The Hippie's Sister	192
57	The Vegas Syndrome	197
58	One Please	200
59	The Beetle That Went Up a Hill and Came Down a Mountain	202

60	The Truth About Lying	205
61	Rotting Bones	208
62	Understanding Amazing Grace	211
63	The Bunny Chauffeur	214
64	Sunday Morning Blowout	219
65	What's That Cross Mean, Mommy?	222
66	An Irreplaceable Role	225
67	The Great Fishing Day	228
68	Michael J. Fox	231
69	Praise	233
70	The Faith That Enron Built	236
71	Free Bandicoot	242
72	Marching Onward in Faith	245
73	Andy's Name	248
74	The Runaway Ferris Wheel	251
75	The Two-Headed Monster	255
76	God's Glory in the Storm	258
77	The Princess Bride	261
78	Need a Lift?	266
79	Never, Ever Plant Mexican Petunias	269
80	Walkabout	272
81	Pleasing Everybody	275
82	Untying the Ribbon	277
83	Seeing God in an Ultrasound	280
84	The Trip Is Bountiful	283
85	The Pinkie Chronicles	289
86	A Garden of Hope	292
87	The Designer Purse	295
88	Road Trips and Righteousness	298
89	Don't Sweat the Small Stuff	301
90	Let It Shine	304

1
Vertically Challenged

For all have sinned and fall short of the glory of God, and all are justified freely by His grace through the redemption that came by Christ Jesus.
Romans 3:23-24 NIV

Years ago, in the youth group in my previous church home, there was a great guy in the group that everyone loved dearly. He had a fantastic sense of humor, a kind heart, and a smile that lit up the room. He was also the shortest male in the group.

He may have tired of being called "cute," but he never showed it. The other guys would occasionally tease him about being short, but he took it all in stride with his good nature.

Then, one day when he was being picked on, he replied with a pearl of wisdom wrapped in humor. He simply said, "We're all the same height at the foot of the cross." Everyone laughed, and then everyone agreed wholeheartedly.

I remember thinking how true that is on so many levels. We've all experienced looking out a window of a tall building to see the people walking below. They look like ants! It's a matter of perspective.

On a deeper level, I thought about how "all have sinned and fall short of the glory of God," (Romans 3:23) and how we need the redemption of a Savior. In essence, we were all "vertically challenged" — we lost our connection to our Father above through our own sin. Doomed to live a horizontal life forever, never having the abundance intended for us, we were in a terribly depressing state of dying. Then, the Lord Almighty made a way for all of us to be restored to a relationship with Him through the sacrifice of His Son on the cross.

Just as sin is no respecter of persons, neither is the saving grace of Jesus Christ. After all, it was a mere thief on a cross next to Jesus to whom He said, "Today, you will be with Me in paradise." What if Jesus had looked at this man's "stature" among his peers — a despicable, dishonest reprobate — and decided he was just too awful to save.

Think of your own sin. Do you see the filth of your own sin before it was washed away in the sacrificial blood of an innocent Man? Are you still comparing your spiritual "height" to others and deeming their sin worse than yours? Judging the hearts of others has been a problem since the fall of man.

As God's royal priesthood, we are not called to a ministry of comparison. We are called to a ministry of completeness in Jesus Christ. We are called to share with those still dying the reconciling love of Christ. How it must grieve God when He sees us bickering, accusing and judging each other's hearts at the foot of the cross rather than falling on our faces before the risen Lord!

Could our sinful state before Christ saved us be equivalent to casting lots for His clothing? Pounding the nails into His wrists? What about the present-day sins we all "rate?" Adultery, pornography, child abuse, fornication — they seem so much uglier than our own "minor" sins. Yet, the sin that sent Jesus to the cross is my own. And your own.

Indeed, we all stand the same height at the foot of the cross before salvation as well as after!

In Thought

"Dear Lord, thank You for Your love for me. That You would die for me alone is more than I can comprehend. Help me not to judge the hearts of others. Show me from whence I came before I accepted Your gift of salvation. Please make me more loving and grateful towards You as well as toward Your children. Thank You that salvation is for all. Amen."

In Word

- *You, my brothers and sisters, were called to be free. But do not use your freedom to indulge the flesh; rather, serve one another humbly in love. For the entire law is fulfilled in keeping this one command: "Love your neighbor as yourself." If you bite and devour each other, watch out or you will be destroyed by each other.* Galatians 5:13-15 NIV
- *Therefore, if anyone is in Christ, he is a new creation; old things have passed away; behold, all things have become new. Now all things are of God, who has reconciled us to Himself through Jesus Christ, and has given us the ministry of reconciliation, that is, that God was in Christ reconciling the world to Himself, not imputing their trespasses to them, and has committed to us the word of reconciliation.* 2 Corinthians 5:17-19 NKJV
- *Now the works of the flesh are evident, which are: adultery, fornication, uncleanness, lewdness, idolatry, sorcery, hatred, contentions, jealousies, outbursts of wrath, selfish ambitions, dissensions, heresies, envy, murders, drunkenness, revelries, and*

the like; of which I tell you beforehand, just as I also told you in time past, that those who practice such things will not inherit the kingdom of God. But the fruit of the Spirit is love, joy, peace, longsuffering, kindness, goodness, faithfulness, gentleness, self-control. Against such there is no law. Galatians 5:19-23 NKJV

In Deed
- Ask the Lord to show you in what ways you have been comparing yourself to others. Ask His forgiveness for those whose hearts you have judged and ask Him to remove your pride.
- Look up Scriptures about your worth in Christ and commit them to memory.

Kim Lindquist

2

The Sweet Spot

*For I know the plans I have for you, declares the LORD,
plans for welfare and not for evil, to give you a future
and a hope.*
Jeremiah 29:11 ESV

"He swings!"

CRACK!

"It's a long, long fly ball to left! No way is the fielder going to reach this one! It's gone!"

I don't need to explain what just happened, do I? Those of us who played the game once upon a time know what it feels like to hit the ball just right. The correct hand/eye coordination, swinging the bat at the perfect speed, the feel you get when the ball hits the bat. You can tell just from the feel of it in your hands and the sound it makes that you nailed it. You hit the bat's sweet spot.

But how many swings did it take to get there? A few? Hundreds? How many did you swing at and miss completely? How many left you just standing there, looking? Through repetition, persistence and patience, you learned what it took. And when everything was right....*CRACK!*

I've been unemployed for an extended period of time. I've been divorced and I've had the bank tell me I couldn't live in my house anymore; it's theirs now. Throughout it all, God picked me up off the ground, dusted me off, and sent me back to the plate. He told me to keep going, but to trust my Coach. I'm deeper in the Word than ever, closer to Him, and more trusting of Him. He has given me a new purpose and I'm finally doing things I only dreamed about before. I'm now a self-employed writer, which means I'm still broke, but not broken.

He had to bring me back to the foot of the cross. He had to bring me back to home plate. And in it I found my sweet spot...and what I need to do to keep it.

The Christian life requires the same attitude.

Practice. Persistence. Patience. Vision. Fall short in any one of these and you find yourself swinging at air much like Paul describes his "shadowboxing" in 1 Corinthians 9:26.

We have to practice the things the Word compels and commands us to do. Prayer. Bible study. Encouraging others. Giving. Loving our neighbor. We must do them regardless of our fickle feelings. If we've been born again, we must have God's vision, not our own, and allow Him to tell us when to "swing." Let the Holy Spirit be your Holy Coach.

He never ever gives up on us. He promises He'll never leave us or forsake us. Those who belong to Him never stray too far. He won't let us. Trials teach us that we have two choices: we'll either run TO Him, or run INTO Him. We'll turn around and return on our own, or He'll step into our paths and say, "That's far enough. I've got you now." The second one is almost always more painful at first....until we find the sweet spot.

In Thought

"Dear Lord, I need to be constantly reminded that I play on *Your* team, not mine. I know You have what I'm going through under control and You have a purpose for it. Help me to keep my eyes on You. Help me to see the big picture. Grant me the patience and vision I long for. Amen."

In Word

- *Trust in the Lord with all your heart, and lean not on your own understanding.* Proverbs 3:5-6 ESV
- *Do you not know that in a race all the runners compete, but only one receives the prize? So run that you may obtain it. Every athlete exercises self-control in all things. They do it to receive a perishable wreath, but we an imperishable. So I do not run aimlessly; I do not box as one beating the air. But I discipline my body and keep it under control, lest after preaching to others I myself should be disqualified.* 1 Corinthians 9:24-27 ESV

In Deed

Get out a notepad and write down your daily routine. Are you "practicing" consistently? When's your quiet time? What are you studying in the Word at home, not at church? What's on your prayer list? Do you have one? Do what a follower of Christ is called to do daily and your sweet spot will become more and more evident.

Dwight Baker

3
He Knows My Voice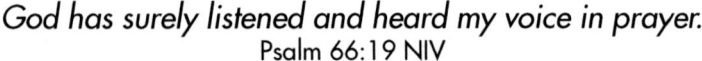

God has surely listened and heard my voice in prayer.
Psalm 66:19 NIV

The fresh piney fragrance of the mountain air hung in the early morning mist as I trudged up the steep pathways that spiraled through camp. Every year my children and I made the drive to the Blue Ridge Mountains of North Carolina to attend a camp where I worked and they played for five weeks. My morning goal was to make three laps along the trail before I began the day at my desk ready to field calls from parents who were missing their children.

As I walked beneath the shelter of tall balsam pines and graceful hemlocks, it was impossible not to feel the presence of God. The mountains surrounded me; their peaks were shrouded in a smoky haze and the slopes layered in shades of blue and green gloriously displaying His workmanship. Distractions faded away and it seemed natural to focus on Him. While exercise was a wonderful way to begin my day, it was this special time alone with God that would truly make or break the long hours ahead.

As the trail wound below the rustic cabins scattered atop the mountain, I began to realize that I wasn't totally alone. Children's chatter floated from the open windows. The morning bugle had blown and breakfast was soon to follow. There's nothing like the cool air of the mountains to awaken one's appetite. Even those who were picky eaters at home found themselves eagerly devouring whatever was offered at camp.

Before breakfast, there was cabin cleanup and each child had chores. I could hear the laughter and excitement of young boys occasionally punctuated by the slamming of a screen door as they worked. Their voices blended together in sweet music to a mother's ears. In the midst of the cacophony I could pick out a familiar voice, the one most important to me, that of my son.

Immediately, I could hear the Lord say to me, "That's exactly how it is with all of My children. My heart is tuned in to every one of them; I can recognize each of their voices. I hear and answer them when they call to Me."

As we go through our days, it is often easy to get caught up in the drama or the drudgery we face. We forget that God longs to be intimately involved with every aspect of our lives whether it's bookkeeping, sales, housework, school or any of the myriad of activities filling the calendar. No matter what occupies the hours and minutes of each day, God is waiting for us to seek His involvement.

Just like the familiar voice that I could hear above all the others, our voices are familiar to our heavenly Father, and He desires for us to speak personally to Him in prayer. He created us for His pleasure which involves an ongoing, two-way relationship with Him. It won't be long until we recognize with certainty His voice as He teaches and instructs us in the way to go. Considering all the voices and noises vying for our attention in this age of electronics, that is an incomparable blessing.

In Thought

"Heavenly Father, I pray that I will seek to establish the habit of being in constant communication with You, the author and the perfecter of my faith. I want to recognize Your voice just as You recognize mine. Amen."

In Word

- *Come and listen, all you who fear God; let me tell you what He has done for me. I cried out to Him with my mouth; His praise was on my tongue. If I had cherished sin in my heart, the Lord would not have listened; but God has surely listened and heard my voice in prayer.* Psalm 66:16-19 NIV
- *My sheep listen to my voice; I know them and they follow me. I give them eternal life and they shall never perish; no one can snatch them out of my hand.* John 10:27-28 NIV
- *For the eyes of the Lord are on the righteous and his ears are attentive to their prayer, but the face of the Lord is against those who do evil.* 1 Peter 3:12 NIV

In Deed

Whether in times of crisis when you are desperate for God's intervention or in everyday situations like searching for a parking place, ask God for His hand to move on your behalf. Remember that He is always available for a heart-to-heart talk. His ears are always open to your cries.

Janie Southard

4

This is My Story

Always be prepared to give an answer to everyone who asks you to give the reason for the hope that you have.
1 Peter 3:15 NIV

Several years ago, I was asked to speak at a fireside event at a retreat. The retreat coordinators had heard me give my testimony in a smaller setting before and wanted me to share it again for their whole group. Honored to do so, I started preparing my notes weeks in advance, but by the Monday night before the retreat, I was at a standstill.

My testimony centered on the death of my mother when I was ten, and it was a story of hope, comfort and joy in the midst of tragedy. The problem was that the message didn't seem to mesh with the current atmosphere or needs of the group to which I'd be speaking. The group was on a "spiritual high" at the time. Everyone was serving. Everyone was eager to learn. And everyone was full of joy. A message of hope, it seemed, was one thing they didn't need at that time.

Frustrated, I called a friend who had heard my testimony several times and expressed my concerns. She assured me that the retreat coordinators who asked me to speak knew exactly what my message would be when they asked, and more importantly, God knew my story as well. "There's a reason why you've been asked to give your testimony," she said, "and it's not your job to figure out the reason. It's just your job to tell your story."

The next morning, I woke up and everything that made no sense the night before became abundantly clear within a matter of hours. It was Tuesday, September 11, 2001. Suddenly the whole world, including those attending the retreat, was in desperate need of a message of hope. And as I spoke to the group around the bonfire that Friday night, I was so thankful that God had prepared me in advance to share my story even though I thought no one needed to hear it.

We all have a story to share. How did you come to know the Lord? What is He doing in your life right now? What are some miracles you've witnessed during your lifetime, and how has He provided for you? Those are your stories. Perhaps you think your story (or your testimony as some call it) isn't dramatic enough. Or maybe you think yours is too dramatic. Stop worrying. It's not your job to question the outcome of sharing your story; it's just your job to tell it.

In John 9, John tells the story of a man who was born blind. Jesus healed him, and after he received his sight, others asked him to explain what had happened. The man didn't have all the answers. He wasn't eloquent, and he couldn't explain exactly how Jesus healed him or where Jesus received His power. All he could do was tell them, in very simple terms, his story. "I know nothing about that one way or the other. But I know one thing for sure: I was blind... I now see" (John 9:25 MSG).

Your personal testimony is one of the greatest tools you have to share Christ with others. It's unique. It's authentic. And it's powerful. You don't have to have all the answers; just tell your story and watch how God is glorified through it!

In Thought

"Dear Lord, thank You for working in my life and for giving me a story to tell. You are called the author of our faith, and it is clear that my life is simply a story You've written in which You've given me the honor of participating. Thank You for every time You've allowed me to share my story with another, and I pray that You will give me many more opportunities to do so again in the future. Amen."

In Word

- *You show that you are a letter from Christ, the result of our ministry, written not with ink but with the Spirit of the living God, not on tablets of stone but on tablets of human hearts.* 2 Corinthians 3:3 NIV
- *But you will receive power when the Holy Spirit comes on you; and you will be my witnesses in Jerusalem, and in all Judea and Samaria, and to the ends of the earth.* Acts 1:8 NIV
- *We are witnesses of these things, and so is the Holy Spirit, whom God has given to those who obey him.* Acts 5:32 NIV

In Deed

- Over the next two weeks, read the book of Acts. Pay attention to the passion with which the first witnesses shared the good news of what Christ had done for them.
- Write out your own personal testimony. You can do it longhand or just put the main points on a 3 x 5 note card to keep in your wallet or purse.
- After you are done, thank God for your story and ask Him for an opportunity to share it with someone. When that opportunity arises, don't overanalyze it; just start talking!

Emily Ryan

21

5
We Okay, Daddy?

Trust in the Lord with all your heart,
and lean not on your own understanding.
Proverbs 3:5 NIV

Last summer, my oldest son, James, turned three years old. My husband, Mike, decided that he was old enough to take him on a boat ride into Galveston Bay, just father and son. Up until this time, someone else had always accompanied them to ensure that James did not fall overboard while Mike drove the boat. Reluctantly, I agreed for them to take the short cruise around the bay that evening while the winds and waters were calm.

I watched anxiously from the patio as he placed our excited son, wearing a bright red lifejacket, into the boat and kept watching until they slipped from my view. It was obvious that James was enjoying his new-found freedom as he darted all over the boat, exploring every inch. I will never forget hearing James' voice above the motor's roar as he prattled on about everything he thought and saw.

I tried to stay busy for the hour they were gone, although I have to admit that I kept glancing out the window each time I heard a boat pass by. Finally, I spotted my men as they glided toward the bay house. I held my breath until I saw that little head bouncing up and down in the bow of the boat. Relief filled my heart as I could not help but run down to the dock to greet them.

"How was the ride?" I asked.

"Great!" James yelled out as his daddy lifted him to the shore. I looked to my husband for his reply.

"James did great!" Mike answered, "Even when we got stuck!"

"What?" I shouted, and began checking my son for signs of bruises or broken bones. It was then I noticed that Mike was wet and caked in mud up to his waist. "What happened?"

He explained that they had been out about thirty minutes and were near Moody Gardens when Mike realized the boat was lunging forward and brown mud was being stirred up by the motor. He tried to steer them out, but it was too late, and they were stuck in an oyster bed.

In order to get free, Mike realized he would have to get out and push while James stayed in the boat. He explained to James what needed to be done, and James nodded that he understood. However, his eyes were huge as Mike took off his shoes and climbed into the muddy water, and he stood in the boat as close to Mike as he could get. Just as Mike began to push the boat, he heard a worried, small voice call out, "We okay, Daddy?"

Mike assured him that they were okay, but a few seconds later, James said again, "We okay, Daddy?"

"Yes, son, we are okay. Just stay right where you are. I am going to take care of you," Mike said, but before he could even finish speaking James asked the same question a third time.

"We okay, Daddy?"

This time Mike looked right into his eyes and held his little hands and calmly said to him, "James, we are going to be just fine. Trust me that I am going to take care of you." With that, James was finally satisfied, not moving or speaking again until the boat was safely headed back home.

23

James not only had to trust his father, he also had to obey and be still while staying in the safety of the boat until the danger had passed. As Christians we are often faced with the same situation: Obey. Be still. Trust our Father.

James does not yet have a full understanding of God, but he knows his daddy will do everything in his power to keep him safe and out of harm's way. We have a Father who will keep us safe as well. The question is, do you trust Him?

As a mother, I know the day will come when James will go out on his own and face the world without the protection of his parents. It is my prayer that he will have learned from his earthly father that he can also place his trust in his heavenly Father even more!

In Thought
"Lord, help me to trust You on a daily basis. Help me to rest in the knowledge that Your ways are higher than mine. You are the Alpha and Omega as well as my heavenly Father who loves me. Amen."

In Word
The Lord is my strength and my shield; my heart trusts in Him, and He helps me. My heart leaps for joy, and with my song I praise Him. Psalm 28:7 NIV

In Deed
Trusting God on a daily basis does not always come naturally. It takes practice, so don't wait. Start today. In humble prayer ask the Lord for help in trusting Him daily to take care of you, your needs, and the direction of your life.

Mikelle Challenger

6
Failing to Forgive

But You are a God of forgiveness, gracious and compassionate, slow to anger, and abounding in lovingkindness; and You did not forsake them.
Nehemiah 9:17 NASB

When I was a young girl, I had a horrible experience at the hands of a drunken man. One day while riding a bus, this man spoke to me and about me in such a vile manner that I became infuriated. My anger was so great that I vowed I would do anything to pay him back for his treatment of me. As the years passed, whenever I would think of my humiliation at his hands I became even angrier—so much so that this man ceased to exist for me. Had he been dying of thirst, I would not have given him a drink. Years later, after I had become a Christian, I encountered him again and the Lord, who is just and merciful, broke my heart over this man.

During my encounter with this nemesis from my past, the Lord made me realize that I had in essence murdered him in the Spirit! This man, for whom Christ had also died, was someone I had allowed the unforgiveness in my heart to kill. I had been a Christian for several years but had never shared Christ with him because of my hatred towards him. After this realization hit me, all I could do was cry out

25

to the Lord to forgive me for my failure. I later went back and asked this man if he knew Christ. He didn't, but he listened as I shared the gospel with him. Although he didn't accept Christ that day, I planted the seed which, perhaps, someone else will harvest.

Often, we allow our feelings to get in the way of the commandment to share the good news of Christ with others. Perhaps, like me, you have had someone humiliate, anger or betray you and you developed an unforgiving attitude. Or maybe an ongoing situation at work or home is making you bitter, angry and frustrated. Whatever the situation, pray for the courage to forgive. Forgiveness is a decision, not an emotion. It is a choice, not a feeling. If we wait to feel like forgiving someone, it will never happen. We must make an active choice to release our anger, pain and bitterness. Forgiveness releases us from the prison of bitterness that holds us in bondage and keeps us from moving forward.

Forgiveness is possible because of the forgiveness we have received through Christ. "Therefore let it be known to you, brethren, that through Him forgiveness of sins is proclaimed to you, and through Him everyone who believes is freed from all things, from which you could not be freed through the Law of Moses." (Acts 13:38-39 NASB).

If you have an unforgiving attitude, remember that we have been forgiven so much more than we can possibly know or conceive by our Savior. His commandment to us is to love our enemies and to pray for those who hate us. Do not allow this failure to forgive to rule and reign in your heart any longer. Decide to follow the example of our Lord and forgive. It will set you free to live, love and serve our Lord as never before.

In Thought

"Dear Jesus, I know that You came, lived and died so that I might be forgiven of my sins. Please give me the courage to forgive those who have offended and hurt me. Help me to follow in Your example of love and forgiveness. Amen."

In Word

- *Then Peter came to Jesus and asked, "Lord, how many times shall I forgive my brother or sister who sins against me? Up to seven times?" Jesus answered, "I tell you, not seven times, but seventy-seven times.* Matthew 18:21-22 NIV
- *When you were dead in your sins and in the uncircumcision of your flesh, God made you alive with Christ. He forgave us all our sins, having canceled the charge of our legal indebtedness, which stood against us and condemned us; he has taken it away, nailing it to the cross.* Colossians 2:13-14 NIV
- *If we confess our sins, he is faithful and just and will forgive us our sins and purify us from all unrighteousness.* 1 John 1:9 NIV

In Deed

- Read the parable of the unmerciful servant in Matthew 18:21-35.
- Make a list of at least ten things for which the Lord has forgiven you.
- Pray that God would help you remember this list any time you are having a hard time forgiving someone else.

Patricia Dixon

7
Perfect Vision

To God belong wisdom and power; counsel and understanding are his.
Job 12:13 NIV

I was young when the eye doctor determined that I needed glasses, and I'll never forget my first day with 20/20 vision. I was amazed at how clear the television looked and fascinated by the fact that I could read the street signs that lined the roadways. It was as if my whole world expanded, and I could see more than I had ever seen before. Lines were crisper. Colors were brighter, and faces were more distinguishable than I knew possible.

I hadn't even realized how poor my vision was until I had something to compare it to, and it wasn't long before my young mind began to imagine the benefits of a whole new world in which I could see everything clearly. Now that I knew how wonderful vision could be with my glasses, I hatched a long-term plan to bring 20/20 vision to every area of my life – even my dreams.

I always thought that my dreams were fuzzy and blurry because of my eyesight, and if I just had perfect vision, I'd be able to see all of my dreams with clarity and understand every last detail. I knew that wearing my new glasses to bed wouldn't help since my eyes would be closed when I slept, but I imagined a day when I'd be able to wear contacts to sleep! My vision, even in sleep, would be corrected and my dreams would no longer be blurry.

I had to wait several years to put my big plan into motion, but at last I received my first pair of contacts. Against the doctor's orders, I carefully chose a special night to "forget" to take them out before bedtime, and I fell asleep anticipating an exciting night of perfect vision in my dreams.

Boy, was I disappointed!

My dreams were just as fuzzy and just as unclear as before, and it wasn't until I broke down and told someone what I'd done that I learned that dreams are, by nature, blurry and out of focus. It seems there are some things that will always remain shrouded in a mysterious, blurry fog regardless of perfect vision.

At times in my spiritual walk, I still find myself expecting and imagining a world in which I can see everything with 20/20 vision as well. When I'm going through a difficult time, I imagine that I will come out on the other side with complete understanding as to why God allowed the trial to happen. When God's plan for my life doesn't seem to make sense, I imagine that if I just read the Bible or pray enough, the day will come when all of the pieces will magically come together, and I'll suddenly understand His will perfectly. After all, don't they say that hindsight is 20/20?

In the book of Job, we can see that this naïve expectation to fully understand God and His ways can fall upon even the most mature believers. Job went through a long, tedious time of suffering and trials, but he seemed to hold on to the fact that someday he would see clearly the reasoning behind the testing. Everywhere he looked, things seemed blurry and didn't make sense. He questioned God. He longed for understanding. And he expected that God would give him the clarity he so desired.

But when God finally answered Job, only one thing became perfectly clear: God did not owe Job a thing! No answers. No explanation. No clarity at all. In fact, He told Job that if anyone was qualified to ask the questions, it was He, not Job. "Brace yourself like a man; I will question you, and you shall answer me," God said in Job 38:3 (NIV).

How many times do we continue to question God just like Job did and naïvely expect that He will answer us according to our own satisfaction? We imagine that He'll give us perfect insight into His divine ways every time, and we forget that there are some times that things will always remain a little blurry. God is God and His ways are higher than our ways. Sometimes He will grant us clarity and perfect vision, and other times He will just keep His ways a mystery. He does not owe us an explanation, nor does He owe us perfect vision, even in hindsight. He is, after all, God. And we are not.

In Thought
"Dear God, Your ways are so much higher than my ways. I have the desire to see everything clearly with Your perfect vision and insight, but I know that You do not owe me an explanation for everything You do. Help me remember that part of understanding You is accepting that there are some things that I will never fully understand. Amen."

In Word
•   *"For my thoughts are not your thoughts, neither are your ways my ways," declares the LORD. "As the heavens are higher than the earth, so are my ways higher than your ways and my thoughts than your thoughts." Isaiah 55:8-9 NIV*

- *Then Job replied to the Lord: "I know that you can do anything, and no one can stop you. You asked, 'Who is this that questions my wisdom with such ignorance?' It is I—and I was talking about things I knew nothing about, things far too wonderful for me." Job 42:1-3 NLT*

In Deed
- Read Job 38-42. Does God ever give Job an explanation for his testing?
- Make a list of questions that you have for God. Then pray over them with the understanding that He may or may not choose to give you the insight you desire.

Emily Ryan

Week 1 Notes

_____

_____

_____

_____

_____

_____

_____

_____

_____

_____

_____

_____

_____

_____

_____

_____

_____

8
Amber's Story

And the King will answer and say to them, "Assuredly I say to you, inasmuch as you did it to one of the least of these My brethren, you did it to Me."
Matthew 25:40 NKJV

Amber Rose was my great niece. It was pure joy to be around her because she always had a smile on her face. Amber was born with the wall between the two lower chambers of her heart missing. Within hours, she was rushed to surgery in the Texas Medical Center, and it was a true miracle that she lived. She had multiple heart surgeries after that first one. Through it all, Amber was a happy child. She always smiled and never complained about her condition. As a youngster, she would be playing with others and suddenly stop and sit down. She would just have to rest for a while. Then she would get back up later and join in playing again. But she never complained. She always thought about others, even when she was a toddler sharing her toys. Amber wanted everyone else to have a good time playing.

As Amber grew older, she valued each day she lived. She knew that her parents had been told when she was born that she probably wouldn't live through the first surgery, and if she did, she probably would not live for longer than maybe five years. So Amber really loved to celebrate birthdays. She had 28 birthday parties on this earth before her Lord Jesus called her home. Yes, Amber Rose loved Jesus. She loved to tell people about Jesus, too.

At Amber's home-going celebration, her fiancé told a story which really gives an insight into Amber's true character. One day, he and Amber were shopping at a local discount chain. They had completed their purchases and were leaving the store. Just outside the door was a homeless man asking for money for some food. Most people would just walk right by the man. A few may give him some coins. Some may even give him a few dollar bills. Not Amber. She took the man back into the store along with her fiancé and she bought the man a whole new set of clothes. Then they took the man to the Olive Garden restaurant and bought him lunch. She also shared with him all about her Savior, Jesus. There must have been background music of an angel chorus at Olive Garden that day. It is a fact that there is a man in this world who believes that he met an angel that day. His life may never be the same because of her acts of kindness toward him. When Amber entered heaven, she was surely greeted by so many who told her, "You touched my life when I needed it," or "You were there when I needed someone," or "You were an angel to me."

How many times do we go through our daily routines and miss opportunities to be a blessing to someone? Even if we think we have a good prayer connection with our Lord, sometimes we are the ones talking and not listening. Prayer is a two-way connection. We are to pray and then listen for direction. Then we are to act on His directions. That is what Amber Rose did with her life. She didn't wait until she was old. She didn't have that much time. She used every minute she had.

Amber's grandmother (my sister) and I both love to grow daylilies. They make a lot of buds and each one blooms for only one day, hence the name—daylily. We like to get daylilies that have been developed as seedlings but are not named. They are cheaper and we like to give them our own special names. My sister named one—you guessed it—Amber Rose. It is a beautiful golden color with a rosy blush on the petals, just like the rosy blush on Amber's cheeks when she smiled. Every May when this flower blooms, I see Amber's rosy cheeks, and I am encouraged to do something beneficial for my fellow man.

Any time golden flowers with rosy petals bloom, think of Amber Rose and what she would do, and then go and do likewise.

In Thought

"Lord, thank You for Amber Rose's life and how You used it for Your kingdom. Help us to learn from her example how to be a witness for You. Help us to live each day to the fullest and not put off until tomorrow what You would have us do today. Amen."

In Word

- A man's heart plans his way. But the Lord directs his steps. Proverbs 16:9 NKJV
- The fruit of the Spirit is love, joy, peace, patience, kindness, goodness, faithfulness. Galatians 5:22 NIV
- I will bless her with abundant provisions; her poor will I satisfy with food. Psalm 132:15 NIV

In Deed

Next time you see someone in need, whether it is a homeless person or someone you know personally, open your heart and perhaps your pocketbook, and think about how you would feel if the roles were reversed and you were the person in need. Just remember, God loves both of you.

Sharon Rigsby

Men's Shoes...
Size 10

And my God will meet all your needs according to the riches of His glory in Christ Jesus.
Philippians 4:19 NIV

Six months after my husband, Mike, and I married, we found ourselves driving to South Florida in a big, yellow truck. With all of our possessions packed into the moving van we had rented, we moved from the Dallas metroplex to the sunny shores of Delray Beach. It was a great move for us because Mike had been laid off the month before and we were starting a new job there. It was scary, though, because we had to start from scratch financially and move over 2,500 miles from both of our families! The following four years were an amazing time of spiritual growth for both of us as we each learned to trust God for all our needs and to lean on Him for everything on a daily basis. One such lesson came in the form of a pair of men's shoes...size 10.

That first year was very lean because we both were committed to living debt free. We knew we could not prevent future job losses, but we could do our best to put ourselves in a position to ride out those storms. We did not buy anything unless it was an absolute necessity. We were able to save a lot of money that way, but it was not easy. One day Mike came out of our bedroom, frustrated, and said, "Mikelle, I need a pair of shoes."

I gave him my pat answer, "Well, let's pray about it and maybe the Lord will provide them so we won't have to spend any money."

He had heard all this before, but this time he was ready for me. "So you mean that we pray about it and the Lord will just provide a stylish pair of men's shoes...size 10?" He did not wait for my response and just left for work.

I felt the gauntlet thrown down, so before I went to work that day I prayed, "Lord, thank You for providing for all our needs in whatever form they come. We are doing our best to be faithful to You and to Your plan for our lives. Lord, please answer our prayer and provide Mike a nice pair of men's shoes...size 10!"

Within a week, we received a pair of custom, Italian leather men's shoes! It amazed us because we had not told anyone of Mike's need for shoes. Inside the box, we found a note from someone we had met only a few times before that read, "I found these and thought Mike might like them." I will never forget the surprise and emotion that came across Mike's face as he reached out and accepted this great gift. Though we should not have been so surprised, we both found ourselves very shocked by this. Those shoes still sit in our closet as a testament to God's faithfulness in our lives, even when our faith wavers at times! Not only were they a stylish pair of men's shoes, yes, you guessed it...they were a size 10!

When was the last time you trusted in the Lord for a need? Isn't it so much easier just to run to the store and buy it or charge it? It's a lot faster at times. But we have taken God out of the equation. He wants to meet our every need, and He will provide in the exact time we need it. Don't miss out on your blessing today. Trust God. He never fails!

In Thought

"Lord, You are the creator of everything, and everything belongs to You. Help me to trust daily in You to provide for all my needs both big and small. Amen."

In Word

- *I have no need of a bull from your stall or of goats from your pens, for every animal of the forest is mine, and the cattle on a thousand hills.* Psalm 50:9-10 NIV
- *Those who know your name trust in you, for you, LORD, have never forsaken those who seek you.* Psalm 9:10 NIV

In Deed

- Go to your local church library or Christian bookstore and find some books about George Mueller, a man who opened an orphanage in the 1800's. He spent over 60 years depending solely on God to meet the needs of the orphans and recorded those needs, along with how they were met, as a testimony of prayer and faith.
- Begin writing down your own needs as you pray for them, and write down how and when God provides for you. Refer to your list of answered prayers often to renew your faith.

Mikelle Challenger

10
What's That Smell?

Do not put out the Spirit's fire; do not treat prophecies with contempt. Test everything. Hold on to the good. Avoid every kind of evil.
1 Thessalonians 5:19-22 NIV

It was winter, so a fire in the fireplace was appropriate. But though my brother and sister and I were enjoying a reprieve from school during the Christmas break, the days were starting to grow long and boring as the cold kept us indoors. One particularly cold day, I found myself reading in my room most of the morning while my brother, who was about four years old at the time, and our cousins played with their toys in the living room.

I was just getting to the climax of my book when something made me stop reading. I dropped the book to my lap and squinted my eyes trying to figure out what was different. Did I hear a noise? Was it getting warmer? Wait…*what was that smell?* I crinkled my nose and tried to analyze the subtle smell that somehow reminded me of s'mores and PE class all at once. For a moment, I contemplated ignoring the smell and getting back to the excitement of my book, but curiosity finally got the best of me and I left the room to investigate.

I met my mom in the hallway, and we both followed our noses to the living room where the campfire/locker room smell seemed to be originating. We inspected the fireplace. Nothing seemed out of place, so she got out the poker and started poking around the logs. In no time at all, she unearthed the remnants of a very small, but very melted, plastic "jelly" shoe. We wondered how in the world one of my jellies had gotten into the fireplace when at once we turned to find my brother and cousins walking down the hall – their arms full of more shoes. It seemed the jelly had just been an experiment to see if, in fact, girls' shoes melted. And note to all – they do!

Have you ever been watching a television show, listening to a sermon, or even receiving advice from a friend, when something suddenly "smelled funny" to you about what you just heard? Maybe you couldn't put your finger on it, but something just seemed out of place or not quite right, and the thought crossed your mind that maybe you should investigate and verify that in the Bible before you took it as 100% truth. Well as it turns out, those "What's that smell?" moments are there for a reason, and you shouldn't ignore your instincts when your spirit questions something you've heard.

In 1 Thessalonians 5:21, we're told to "test everything" according to God's Word. That means that if we read or hear a message that claims to be from God, we have a responsibility to investigate and see if that message aligns with the Bible or not.

Of course, most of us are not Bible scholars. We have a general foundation of the Scriptures, but not enough to declare ourselves experts in the fields of biblical theology or doctrine. If that's the case, how are we ever to know if what we're taught accurately follows God's Word or not?

That's when the "smell test" can come in handy. Many times, the Holy Spirit will prompt our hearts just enough to put a question mark in our minds when we hear something that warrants further investigation.

That prompting of the Holy Spirit is not to be ignored.

The book of Acts tells of the Bereans who sat under the teachings of Paul. Every day they took what they heard from Paul and tested it against the Scriptures to see if his message was true or not, and they were commended for their discernment (Acts 17). What about you? Do you examine the preachers you hear or the books you read against the Bible? Or do you just take everything at face value and assume it's accurate without examining it yourself? God gave us the ultimate authority (the Bible) for a reason. Read it. Study it. And test everything according to it. Over time, your nose will become even more sensitive to the "smells" around you, and your sense of discernment will be heightened.

In Thought

"Dear Lord, thank You for Your Spirit that prompts and urges my heart to seek wisdom. I pray You would help me discern everything I hear and that I would test everything according to Your Word. Amen."

In Word

- *Dear friends, do not believe every spirit, but test the spirits to see whether they are from God, because many false prophets have gone out into the world.* 1 John 4:1 NIV
- *I am your servant; give me discernment that I may understand your statutes.* Psalm 119:125 NIV
- *Anyone who lives on milk, being still an infant, is not acquainted with the teaching about righteousness. But solid food is for the mature, who by constant use have trained themselves to distinguish good from evil.* Hebrews 5:13-14 NIV
- *Now the Bereans were of more noble character than the Thessalonians, for they received the message with great*

eagerness and examined the Scriptures every day to see if what Paul said was true. Acts 17:11 NIV

In Deed

- The next time you hear a sermon, take diligent notes. Then go over those notes at home, paying careful attention to the Scriptures that were referenced and the context of the verses.
- When you seek a friend's wisdom for a particular situation, don't be afraid to ask for the biblical backup behind their advice.

Emily Ryan

11
You Said That Last Night!

But above all, my brothers, do not swear, either by heaven or by earth or by any other oath, but let your "yes" be yes and your "no" be no, so that you may not fall under condemnation.
James 5:12 ESV

"Kids say the darndest things." That was the title of Art Linkletter's radio show long ago. If you're a parent or grandparent, you certainly know the phrase is absolutely true.

The other night while sitting with my notepad trying to come up with ideas for this devotional book, lo and behold my own 11-year-old son gave me a gem.

You see, we're trying to get our family back in the habit of eating together every night at the dinner table. At the given time, the TV goes off, kids come in from outside or put their video games down, mom wipes her brow after preparing the meal, and I stop pretending to be working hard on the computer long enough for us to eat together, enjoy each other's company, and talk about our day.

As you can imagine, when you've been inconsistent about it for a while, it's hard to get back in the habit, especially in these times when everyone in the family seems to have different priorities and conflicting events vying for our time. So we decided we needed to make dinner time "family time" again.

But now and then, we either get lazy or hurried or just give in to the "cafeteria style" dinner where we fill our plates and go their separate ways. This happened on the particular night my son spoke up. I was complaining again, saying, "we need to get back to eating at the table." That's when my son said it:

"Dad, you said that *last* night."

Ugh. He got me. I'd love to say I was embarrassed enough to tell everyone to get to the table.....but no. I let it slide.

I'm sure you can relate to some degree. Maybe not about something so seemingly insignificant, but perhaps another situation where your good intentions don't come to completion. You promised your son you'd finally make it to his baseball game. Taking your daughter to that place she's been begging you to take her keeps getting postponed. That report you promised your boss a week ago is still in draft form.

Christians are expected to be people whose words can be trusted. When James challenges us to let our "yes" be "yes" and our "no" be "no," he's echoing Jesus' teachings in the Sermon on the Mount in Matthew 5:33-37 (see below).

Who expects this of us, aside from the Lord? The short answer is: Everyone. We're all lied to on a daily basis by others through advertising, etc. To be a "man of your word" seems to be from some bygone era. A man's word used to be his bond. A handshake used to "seal the deal." Not anymore, at least that's what the cynical in the world believe; and for the most part, they're right.

Being that kind of person others can depend on to "walk the walk" alone sets us apart from the world. There's much more to the Christian life than just that, but it's a great start. It's the least we can do.

Now, if you'll forgive me, I have to stop writing now. It's dinner time.

In Thought

"Dear heavenly Father, I long to be a person who keeps his word. By my very actions and speech, I represent You in everything I do. I need to be a trustworthy person and do what I say I'm going to do. I don't want to just talk the talk; help me to walk the walk. Amen."

In Word

Again you have heard that it was said to those of old, "You shall not swear falsely, but shall perform to the Lord what you have sworn." But I say to you, "Do not take an oath at all, either by heaven, for it is the throne of God, or by the earth, for it is his footstool, or by Jerusalem, for it is the city of the great King. And do not take an oath by your head, for you cannot make one hair white or black. Let what you say be simply 'Yes' or 'No'; anything more than this comes from evil."
Matthew 5:33-37 ESV

In Deed

Test yourself. Are you trustworthy? Do you keep your word? Take a notepad with you this week and write down every time you make a promise to someone whether it is returning a phone call, doing that task your spouse asked you to do, or spending time with your child. At the end of the week, see how many promises were kept and how many were broken.

Dwight Baker

12

Sharing Our Life Saver

*Therefore comfort each other and edify one another,
just as you also are doing.*
1 Thessalonians 5:11 NKJV

In 2005, soon after Hurricane Katrina struck the Gulf Coast, I happened to see a cartoon drawing of a man rescuing another man from the sea. The picture was not drawn with that event in mind, but it quickly reminded me of all that was being done to help those affected by the storm.

According to the National Oceanic and Atmospheric Administration as written on the website of the National Climatic Data Center, "Hurricane Katrina was one of the strongest storms to impact the coast of the United States during the last 100 years. With sustained winds during landfall of 125 mph (a strong category 3 hurricane on the Saffir-Simpson scale) and minimum central pressure the third lowest on record at landfall (920 mb), Katrina caused widespread devastation along the central Gulf Coast states of the US. Cities such as New Orleans, LA, Mobile, AL, and Gulfport, MS bore the brunt of Katrina's force and will need weeks and months of recovery efforts to restore normality."

Houstonians were flocking to the old Astrodome and other facilities to help refugees from New Orleans as well as other cities. It was unbelievable to see just how many had to flee from their homes to a "foreign land," in a sense.

Since then, I have met many lovely people who relocated permanently to the Houston area as a result of Katrina. Some are now our neighbors, our teachers, and our fellow church members.

We sometimes have our own storms...the surging waves of living in a fallen world that pummel us in cyclic rhythm, the rising waters of our daily responsibilities, the fatigue from treading water as we sometimes feel we've made no progress in our lives, and the mighty winds of troubles that strive to knock us off our feet.

Just as we saw our community reach out to the families affected by Katrina, we are called to the same sense of responsibility within the community of our brothers and sisters in Christ. We are all "misplaced" in that we are "foreigners and exiles" (1 Peter 2:11). We need each other as we wait to go to our home in heaven.

> *Two are better than one, because they have a good reward for their labor. For if they fall, one will lift up his companion. But woe to him who is alone when he falls, for he has no one to help him up. Again, if two lie down together, they will keep warm; but how can one be warm alone? Though one may be overpowered by another, two can withstand him. And a threefold cord is not quickly broken.*
> Ecclesiastes 4:9-12 NKJV.

We must share the love of Jesus, our life preserver, with those who are in the midst of a storm - share the truth of God's Word, meet tangible needs, pray with them, point them back to Christ, and show them the love of the Father. As we know, those who are in the "eye" of the storm have already passed through the harshness of the storm...and will pass through it again. When we find ourselves in the "eye" of our storms, enjoying a time of fewer troubles, we can use that time to reach out to others being battered by the wind and waves.

In Thought

"Lord, thank You for carrying us during our times of affliction. Please help us to keep our eyes on You during those times. Give us opportunities to help others who are suffering, and lead me to share with those who do not yet know You as their life saver. Amen."

In Word

- *For as we have many members in one body, but all the members do not have the same function, so we, being many, are one body in Christ, and individually members of one another.* Romans 12:4-5 NKJV
- *Be kindly affectionate to one another with brotherly love, in honor giving preference to one another; not lagging in diligence, fervent in spirit, serving the Lord; rejoicing in hope, patient in tribulation, continuing steadfastly in prayer; distributing to the needs of the saints, given to hospitality.* Romans 12:10-13 NKJV
- *Now we exhort you, brethren, warn those who are unruly, comfort the fainthearted, uphold the weak, be patient with all.* 1 Thessalonians 5:14 NKJV

In Deed

Spend time in God's Word today. Ask Him to reveal to you what He wants to teach you today. Then pray that He will show you who to reach out to with His love.

Kim Lindquist

13
White as Snow

"Come now, let's settle this," says the Lord. "Though your sins are like scarlet, I will make them as white as snow. Though they are red like crimson, I will make them as white as wool."
Isaiah 1:18 NLT

When my oldest son was six years old, he wrote on the entire side of my vehicle with a Coke tab! He didn't even tell me he did this; I just discovered it one day when the light hit it just right. He had written his name and his older sister's name and then finished off the masterpiece with some squiggly lines.

A few years later when he was eight, the same child started a fire in the kitchen trash because he wanted to see what would happen. Luckily he screamed before it got too big and I was able to put it out without any damage or anyone getting hurt.

Parents are often caught off guard like I was, by our children's "experiments," and most of the time our first reaction is to respond in anger. Maybe we yell. Maybe we give the silent treatment. Maybe we throw an adult version of a temper tantrum. We know we need to forgive, but most of the time that step comes later – almost as an afterthought.

I love that Christ does not respond to our sin in the same way that we respond to that of our children. His first response is love. He forgave us for all of our sins when He died on the cross and His blood washed us white as snow. Of course He still disciplines us when we sin and He still allows us to face the consequences of our actions. But He never responds in anger. He doesn't yell. He doesn't give the silent treatment. And He doesn't throw His own temper tantrum when we go astray. Instead He just loves us and waits patiently for us to turn back towards Him.

In Thought

"Dear heavenly Father, thank You so much for loving me and washing away my sins, no matter how deep they were. You took away my scars of sin by having to endure Your own scars and pain just so I could be made as white as freshly fallen snow. I pray that I continue to show this kind of forgiveness and love for others so that You can be exalted. Amen."

In Word

- *The LORD is slow to anger, abounding in love and forgiving sin and rebellion.* Numbers 14:18a NIV
- *When we were overwhelmed by sins, you forgave our transgressions.* Psalm 65:3 NIV
- *The Lord our God is merciful and forgiving, even though we have rebelled against him.* Daniel 9:9 NIV
- *For if you forgive men when they sin against you, your heavenly Father will also forgive you.* Matthew 6:14 NIV

In Deed

The next time someone sins against you, stop and consider what Christ did for you on the cross. Remember that He paid the ultimate sacrifice to cover not only your sin, but the sin of others as well. Before you respond in anger, ask yourself, "If God can love and forgive this person, why can't I?"

Cindy Cañas

14
Undignified

David, wearing a linen ephod, danced before the LORD with all his might, while he and the entire house of Israel brought up the ark of the LORD with shouts and the sound of trumpets.
2 Samuel 6:14-15 NIV

I'll admit, I don't "get" football.

Oh, I understand the game well enough. Two teams of very large and very fast men shroud themselves in padded clothing, slap each other on the backside, then set out to be the best at getting an oblong ball from one end of a field to another by out-running, out-throwing, and out-tackling the other team. The scoring, the rules, the strategy – everything that happens on the field makes plenty of sense even to my feminine mind, especially when filtered through the animated commentary of ESPN sportscasters.

But what I don't get is what happens *off* the field.

I don't understand the fans. I don't understand the exorbitant amounts of money spent on tickets to playoff games. I don't understand the "man caves" devoted to favorite teams. And I don't understand big foam fingers, shaved heads, painted faces, or the complete and utter insanity that otherwise mature men can display during victory celebrations. When I watch grown men with wide eyes and tongues sticking out of their mouths making spectacles of themselves on camera, I get a little embarrassed for them and silently wonder if their wives are watching from home and hanging their heads in humiliation.

"Get a hold of your husbands, ladies," I want to yell, but never would. "Can't you get them to stop acting so… *undignified*?"

However, as it turns out, there is a time and a place for undignified behavior. For inhibitions to fall to the wayside and for typically improper behavior to become temporarily acceptable. For music to become louder. For high-fives to become higher. For celebrations to become… *parties*.

King David – the shepherd-turned-king, man-after-God's-own-heart – was once as undignified as a face-painted football fanatic on the 50-yard line on Super Bowl Sunday.

When the Ark of the Covenant, which was God's venue through which He graced the Israelites with His very presence, was brought back to Jerusalem in 2 Samuel 6, the Bible says that King David celebrated *with all his might.*

There was singing, dancing, eating, leaping, shouting and even (shhh…) disrobing! Scandalous, I know. And though disrobing down to his linen ephod sounds more revealing than it actually was, it was still a typically improper way to be seen in public.

Needless to say, David's wife was not pleased.

But David knew the significance of bringing the Ark back to Jerusalem. The Ark was synonymous with God's presence. With His will. With His protection and His blessing over the nation of

Israel. By celebrating the return of the Ark, he was celebrating Israel's relationship with God. To jump and shout and sing and dance with no inhibitions and no qualms about propriety was simply a natural response to the supernatural influence of the Lord upon his heart.

And so he celebrated. With all his might.

Do you celebrate the Lord like David did? Do I? Or does a bowl game in overtime get you more fired up? Or your children's dance recital? Or a commission on a big sell? Or your engagement? Your retirement? Your remission? Your grandchildren?

God allows us to enjoy many things, but do we enjoy *Him*?

I will probably never shave my head for VBS or paint my face pink to celebrate the spiritual growth in my Bible study class, but I pray that, like David, "I will celebrate before the Lord." And, maybe, just maybe, "I will become even more undignified than this" (2 Samuel 6:21-22 NIV).

In Thought

"Dear Lord, hallelujah! Praise Your name! You are mighty! You are awesome! You amaze me and awe me just by being You! Thank You for Your unconditional love! Thank You for Your never-ending grace! And quench my inhibitions when all I want to do is shout about Your holiness! Amen."

In Word

- *I will praise you as long as I live, and in your name I will lift up my hands.* Psalm 63:4 NIV
- *I will sing to the LORD all my life; I will sing praise to my God as*

long as I live. Psalm 104:33 NIV
- *Let them praise his name with dancing and make music to him with tambourine and harp.* Psalm 149:3 NIV

In Deed

The next time you feel like worshipping God in an "unconventional" way, don't second guess your desires or let the actions of those around you dictate your personal style. Just follow through. It could be as simple as standing when others are sitting, raising your hands, clapping, shouting "Amen!" or just bowing your head in worship.

Emily Ryan

Week 2 Notes

15
A Believing Heart

And Jesus answered and said to them, "Truly, I say to you, if you have faith, and do not doubt, you will not only do what was done to the fig tree, but even if you say to this mountain, 'Be taken up and cast into the sea,' it shall happen. And all things you ask in prayer, believing, you shall receive."
Matthew 21:21-22 NASB

Marilyn was a Christian, but she had a sincere problem with unbelief. She found it hard to stop worrying about everything and trust God to handle her problems. She worried constantly. Marilyn wandered for years in despair questioning if she was truly a Christian because of her unbelieving heart.

Eventually, Marilyn's father became ill with terminal cancer. Marilyn was sitting at his bedside crying when he opened his eyes and smiled at her. "Don't worry for me," he said. "My Father knows me well and has a place prepared for me. We'll be together again when it's your time to come home." It was her father's absolute belief in the final moments of his life that opened Marilyn's eyes. She got to see real faith in action. Her father's calm certainty that they would be reunited in heaven with her mother who had passed away years before was the example Marilyn needed to help her fully trust God.

Marilyn wanted what we all want – tangible proof that our problems will be taken care of. Marilyn's faith prior to her father's death had been weak, and when she prayed, it was without the faith that Christ says is necessary for our prayers to be effective.

Many of us are like Marilyn. We come to Christ with sincere hearts when we first meet Him at the foot of the Cross, but then old attitudes, ideas and behavior keep us rationalizing our circumstances. When we come to Christ, we are supposed to open the doors of our hearts to Him and close them firmly behind Him, allowing nothing of this world to interfere with our faith.

Trust, like forgiveness, is a decision we make. Do we believe Christ is who He says He is? Are we living like we believe Him? We, like Marilyn, have to challenge all of our thoughts to see if they are aligned with the will of God. We are to "demolish arguments and every pretension that sets itself up against the knowledge of God," and "take captive every thought to make it obedient to Christ" (2 Corinthians 10:5 NIV).

Are you walking in unbelief today? Unbelief does not have to be a stronghold in your life. As always, God is there to help you. Ask Him to forgive you for your unbelieving attitudes and decisions. Then, seek Him in His Word; all the answers are found there. He will help you conquer unbelief, answer the questions of your heart, and give you a new outlook on life.

In Thought

"Father in heaven, please forgive me for the sin of unbelief in my life. Increase my trust and faith that I might be like the woman in the Bible who believed that if she could just touch the hem of Jesus' garment, she would be made whole. Your Word says that she was made whole in that instant. Make me whole today. Fill me with a hunger and thirst for Your Word and renew my mind daily. Amen."

In Word

- *The father instantly cried out, "I do believe, but help me overcome my unbelief!"* Mark 9:24 NLT
- *See to it, brothers, that none of you has a sinful, unbelieving heart that turns away from the living God. But encourage one another daily, as long as it is called "Today," so that none of you may be hardened by sin's deceitfulness. We have come to share in Christ, if indeed we hold our original conviction firmly to the very end.* Hebrews 3:12-14 NIV

In Deed

- Set aside time to pray each morning before leaving to start your day and at various times throughout the day, especially when under stress.
- Memorize and meditate on passages of the Bible, and when doubts come, quote your favorite Scriptures.

Patricia Dixon

16
A Wedding
and a Funeral

*Lord, you know the hopes of the helpless. Surely you will
hear their cries and comfort them.*
Psalm 10:17 NLT

Exhaustion didn't even begin to describe the way I felt as I trudged
to the lake, my slow steps matching the heaviness in my heart. I had
retreated to the piney woods of northeast Texas to rest and refocus.
In the previous year, I had watched my father slowly slip away with
congestive heart failure and then boarded a roller coaster of despair
with my widowed mother. Though the whole family was missing
Daddy deeply, she was inconsolable.

In the midst of our grief, my daughter's wedding, scheduled more
than a year before, became the focus. For months we marched to
the steady staccato beat of busyness and commitments. Shopping for
dresses and decorations brought a welcome diversion from the deep
sadness that had shrouded our hearts, and we began to smile again.
Spring arrived and with the wedding day just weeks away we reveled
in a season of celebration. It was pure joy to be surrounded by family
and friends as we shared the happiness of Jenna's special day. As I
saw her beaming face turned toward her groom, I remembered the
day of her birth and the prayers lifted up to a faithful God who had
brought us to this place.

But now the soft warmth of spring had been replaced by the sweltering heat of summer and I was wilting once again. The joys of spring were quickly forgotten as I returned to the aching sorrow of loss and meeting the needs of an elderly parent. But in His constant faithfulness God called me to step away from my agenda and spend time with Him. I began to arrange my schedule to carve out time to read my Bible more often and to spend time in prayer.

While it's easy for a busy wife and mother to plan the activities of home and family, getting away by herself is a nearly insurmountable task. But I had managed to find a few days to get away and I sat in the relative cool of a fading summer day. Though I was a hundred miles from home, I hadn't really left. As I looked out on the expanse of the gently undulating lake, clouds boiled up along the horizon, and I was sorely disappointed to think my precious time away would be marred by rain. But I continued to read and pray hoping I wouldn't be caught in a shower before sunset.

As the sun slowly descended, it became a huge pink and orange circle that dipped itself in the lake, bedazzling its ripples with sparkling light. The sky was bright with a deep magenta glow that backlit each gray cloud with edges of bright white. It was an incredible display of artistry - a priceless gift from my Father in heaven who poured love and strength into my weary soul. And with it came His quiet voice gently explaining to me that it was the billowing clouds on the horizon that made the sunset truly breathtaking. The connection was immediate and undeniable. The deep sorrow of my dad's life ending had indeed made the joy of seeing new lives beginning in a lovely wedding so satisfying.

Although the usual ups and downs of life are not always such a sharp contrast as they had been for me the past few months, the stresses of twenty-first century life certainly take a toll on us. In the midst of it all, God offers comfort and peace and rest to us, but hastily uttered prayers while driving down the freeway are not enough. We must choose to spend some alone time with our Father. It is in those quiet times with Him that we will find that our path is always well lit by God's Word, and His faithfulness never fails.

In Thought

"Lord, when I feel weary and unable to go on, please draw me close and help me to make the effort to get away with You. You are the only true refreshment to my soul and in Your Word is the hope that I need. Thank You for Your faithfulness and Your steadfast love. It never fails me. Amen."

In Word

- *Sing for joy, O heavens! Rejoice, O earth! Burst into song, O mountains! For the Lord has comforted his people and will have compassion on them in their suffering.* Isaiah 49:13 NLT
- *All praise to God, the Father of our Lord Jesus Christ. God is our merciful Father and the source of all comfort. He comforts us in all our troubles, so that we can comfort others.* 2 Corinthians 1:3-4 NLT

In Deed

- Try getting up a half hour earlier to spend time praying and reading God's Word.
- Schedule a full or half day away from work and use the time to reconnect with God.
- Read your Bible while outside. You'll benefit from the change in scenery.

Janie Southard

17
In Cinderella's Shadow

We are all infected and impure with sin. When we display our righteous deeds, they are nothing but filthy rags.
Isaiah 64:6a NLT

During our most recent trip to Disney World, one of the events I most anticipated was a late-night dinner in Cinderella's beautiful castle. Because I was expecting our daughter at the time, I wasn't able to enjoy all of the rides and excursions that are usually so much fun, so I knew the castle visit would be the highlight of my trip.

Since we'd be taking a lot of pictures that evening, I tried to dress a little nicer for dinner than I had during the day. After all, it's not every day that you get to rub shoulders with princesses and dine in a castle, so I didn't want to look as if I'd been walking around in the September heat all day.

The big moment came and it was everything I imagined it would be. The inside of the castle was breathtaking, and Cinderella herself talked and took photos with us while we waited to be seated. She commented about our long "carriage ride" from Texas and shared home-decorating tips from her elaborate castle (apparently, it's all about having pet mice to help with the work!). Then I watched as she doted over my two "little princes" and taught a little girl how to properly twirl and curtsey.

Later, as we ate our supper just as the fireworks show lit up the sky outside the windows of the castle, I knew nothing could spoil this magical evening.

I was wrong.

As we left, our waitress gave us a commemorative folder that held the pictures we'd taken with Cinderella earlier that night, and the minute I looked at the photos, my magical evening disappeared into a puff of ugly reality almost as if the clock had just struck midnight.

Next to Cinderella, I looked like an ugly step sister! While she stood tall and thin with a beautiful ball gown and perfect hair, I was short and round with swollen ankles, wrinkled clothes, and hair that had succumbed to the Florida humidity. Her skin was flawless, her smile inviting, and even her gloved hands looked as if they had been professionally positioned for every shot. Meanwhile, my face was red and splotchy from several days in the sun, my mismatched mommy-bag hung awkwardly across my giant middle, and my "glass slippers" were my ugly brown Crocs.

Before I saw myself in Cinderella's shadow, I had been pretty confident of my appearance. I knew I wasn't "princess material," but at least I felt passable. But when I stood next to true beauty (albeit Disney magic beauty), I saw myself for what I really looked like – a tired mommy in desperate need of a fairy godmother!

Sometimes we can get caught up in how we look spiritually as opposed to those who are not as mature in their faith, and we can become pretty confident in our own righteous appearance. But the

Bible says that our righteousness is like "filthy rags," and that's a truth we sometimes forget when we compare ourselves to others. Perhaps we tithe more than our neighbors, read our Bibles more than our coworkers, or volunteer more than some of our friends. On the surface, we feel great! We may even go so far as to metaphorically pat ourselves on the back and congratulate ourselves on how "holy" we have become.

But the day will come when we stand next to the One who truly is holy, and that's when our own righteousness will be revealed for what it truly is. Filth. Dirt. Rags. Sin. Next to Christ, we are nothing but worn-out tourists standing next to a flawless Cinderella. There is no comparison.

Thankfully, not all hope is lost. When Jesus died on the cross, He exchanged His own royal robes of righteousness for our filthy rags of sin. And when we accept that marvelous display of love, our filthiness disappears, and we become the righteousness of Christ! No fairy godmother needed!

In Thought

"Dear Lord, please forgive me for the times when I get spiritually cocky and forgetful of my own sin. Thank You for paying for my sins on the cross and for exchanging my filth for Your righteousness. Keep me from becoming proud in my spiritual walk and help me always remember what I would look like if not for Your righteousness."

In Word

- *For all have sinned and fall short of the glory of God.* Romans 3:23 NIV
- *Since they did not know the righteousness that comes from God*

and sought to establish their own, they did not submit to God's righteousness. Romans 10:3 NIV
- *God made him who had no sin to be sin for us, so that in him we might become the righteousness of God.* 2 Corinthians 5:21 NIV
- *And by that will, we have been made holy through the sacrifice of the body of Jesus Christ once for all.* Hebrews 10:10 NIV

In Deed
- Read Luke 18:9-14 which is written to those "who were confident of their own righteousness." To whom do you relate more – the Pharisee or the tax collector?
- What did the tax collector say (v. 13), and why did he go home justified before God (v. 14)?
- What can you do differently to be more like the tax collector?

Emily Ryan

18
Freedom to Say His Name

When you pass through the waters, I will be with you; and when you pass through the rivers, they will not sweep over you. When you walk through the fire, you will not be burned; the flames will not set you ablaze.
Isaiah 43:2 NIV

Have you ever thought about what it would be like to live in a place where you were not free to say the name of Jesus? What if, when you made a decision to be an open follower of Jesus where you lived, you faced the certainty of imprisonment and torture? A group of believers I traveled with once met some people who faced that dilemma on a daily basis.

In the dark of night, a man came to a secret meeting place in a country where His Name cannot be spoken. We gathered late and he came dressed in disguise. Our host washed our visitor's feet, and we all shared communion. It was a time that tied our hearts together.   The man shared his story with us. He had learned about Jesus by listening to a radio station originating in another country very far away. He had accepted Jesus as his Savior and was so excited that he went about telling everyone he saw about Jesus. It did not take long before he was turned in to the authorities. His family disowned him, and he was put into prison and tortured. He was repeatedly told to deny Jesus. He would not. He was eventually released when they asked the question, "Do you finally see the light?" which he interpreted "Do you finally see the Light?" and he could truthfully say, "Yes."

He still walks with a limp but does not complain. His only desire is to tell others about Jesus. It breaks his heart that he cannot openly share with others what is in his heart. The authorities watch him closely, so he must be very careful. We shared our experiences with him for about two hours which went by very quickly. We encouraged him as best we could, knowing that any chance he had to spend time with fellow believers was a rare blessing for him.

The next night we met with two brothers who were new believers. One had heard about Jesus on the radio like the man the night before and had accepted Jesus as Savior. He then went and told his brother who accepted Jesus also. They were disowned by their family and ran the risk of being turned in to the authorities by their family. They were young and had a great desire to share Jesus with others. They said, "It is dark on the outside where we live, but it is light inside us."

The following night we had another meeting with a man who was a personal friend of some in our group. It was a precious time of reunion. This man had also recently been released from prison, and his story was much like the first man's. He also desired to tell people about Jesus.

Some of us have been Christians for a long time. For others, it may still be a new way of life. Hopefully you new believers still have that excitement that makes you want to share Jesus with everyone you meet. Those of us who have been believers for a long time sometimes get in a rut and forget what it was like in the beginning. We have to remember that each day is a new day to share Jesus with someone and that we actually have the freedom in this country to do that. We must never take that for granted.

In Thought

"Lord, thank You for Jesus and thank You for the freedom we have in this country to say His name. Help me to be bold and share Jesus with others. Amen."

In Word

- *God is our refuge and strength, an ever present help in trouble.* Psalm 46:1 NIV
- *So we say with confidence, "The Lord is my helper; I will not be afraid. What can man do to me?"* Hebrews 13:6 NIV
- *Those who know your name will trust in you, for you, Lord, have never forsaken those who seek you.* Psalm 9:10 NIV

In Deed

- Consider going on a short-term mission trip with your local church or mission organization.
- If you are unable to do so at this time, get a list of a few missionaries who are going on a trip and pray for them daily while they are away. When they return, invite them over for coffee or dinner to hear about their journey.
- Remember, everyone should be involved in mission work in at least one of three ways: praying, giving or going. If you're not doing at least one of these things, start today.

Sharon Rigsby

19
The Dark Years

When you go out to fight your enemies and you face horses and chariots and an army greater than your own, do not be afraid. The LORD your God, who brought you safely out of Egypt, is with you!
Deuteronomy 20:1 NIV

I like for things to be in order with everything organized and in its rightful place at all times. You could stop by my house on any given day and never know that we have four children and a cat. You may find some dust, but never clutter. I have what is diagnosed as "symmetrical obsessive compulsive disorder" which means that I am that person who will go around straightening pictures and pillows that aren't straight or rearranging chairs if they're not pushed in all the way. My closet is arranged by color and then from short sleeves to long sleeves. Order comes naturally to me.

The flip side is that along with this penchant for order can come much anxiety which can lead to depression. When my second child was born I already had a three-year-old. Nevertheless, I still tried to make sure everything was always in order and even went so far as to iron my baby's burp cloths.

When my youngest was three months old, I finally got to a point where trying to keep up with so much perfectionism took over my mental stability and I had a nervous breakdown. I remember calling my mom crying and asking if I could bring the kids to her house so I could go to the doctor. While sitting in the waiting room, I had no shame in crying. I did not care at all what people thought and I just felt like I was going out of my mind. I honestly felt "crazy."

The doctor was very sensitive to my feelings and assured me that I was still sane; I just had a lot of anxiety. For about nine years I took medication for my anxiety and depression and was able to function much easier. However, about eight months ago my husband was laid off from his job, so we lost our health insurance. Not able to continue my medication, I figured it was as good a time as any to turn to God in a new way and depend solely on Him for healing and patience.

How has it been so far? Amazing! There have been a few times that I have felt overwhelmed, but I step back and let God take control. It will take awhile before I am completely healed – it takes much therapy to get over an obsessive compulsive disorder – but by putting God in the pilot's seat, I am learning to trust Him completely and lean on Him for my anxiety.

Are you feeling overwhelmed or anxious? God puts doctors in our lives to help us through our physical and mental illnesses, but He never wants to be left out of the healing process altogether. He is, after all, the Great Physician.

In Thought

"Oh Lord, You are my mighty physician, and I am so grateful that You are with me in my darkest hours. I pray that I will look to You for healing and that You will heal me in Your perfect timing. I love You and can't wait for the day I meet with You in heaven and are rid of all our suffering. Amen."

In Word

- *Even though I walk through the dark valley of death, I will not be afraid, for you are close beside me. Your rod and your staff protect and comfort me.* Psalm 23:4 NIV
- *He will shelter Israel from the storm and the wind. He will refresh her as a river in the desert and as the cool shadow of a large rock in a hot and weary land.* Isaiah 32:2 NIV
- *Don't worry about anything; instead, pray about everything.* Philippians 4:6a NIV
- *With this news, strengthen those who have tired hands, and encourage those who have weak knees. Say to those who are afraid, "Be strong, and do not fear, for your God is coming to destroy your enemies. He is coming to save you."* Isaiah 35:3-4 NIV

In Deed

When you start to feel yourself being drawn under the deep ocean or lying in a pit with no feeling of hope to get out, read the book of Ephesians. You will find strength and encouragement to take each day one step at a time.

Cindy Cañas

20
Angel in Grandmother's Clothing

Dear children, let us not love with words or tongue but with actions and in truth.
1 John 3:18 NIV

I used to have a picture-perfect idea of what Sunday mornings would look like once I had a family of my own. My husband and I would walk hand in hand through the parking lot to church while our children would follow behind in their matching outfits, quizzing each other on their Bible memory verses and teasing each other about who got to give the offering that day.

Instead, since my husband has to be at church earlier than the rest of us, it's more of a frantic solo race each week as I try to juggle children, diaper bags, Bibles, a purse, and who-knows-what-else through the parking lot while desperately praying I make it to Bible study class before the coffee runs out.

Now imagine what happens when it's raining.

One Sunday morning, it was doing just that, so on top of the usual circus-like juggling, I was trying to fit me and my two boys under my son's tiny, lime green VeggieTales umbrella as we sprinted from the minivan to the shuttle bus that would take us from the far parking lot to the children's building.

We climbed onto the bus, and as we shook like three drenched puppies coming in from the rain, God sent an angel in grandmother's clothing to sweep in, make it all better, and change my expectations of Sunday mornings.

I didn't even see the woman at first. I just felt someone take my bag and my purse from my shoulder and saw a sweet, wrinkled hand lead my older son to the first available seat. "Here, Sweetie, let me help you!" she said, after she'd already helped immensely. She took my umbrella and closed it, sat me down next to my son. I half expected her to offer me milk and cookies with the way she turned chaos into peace in about fifteen seconds flat.

The peace didn't last, of course. "Uh oh, Mom. Canaan's missing a shoe!" my older son said.

Immediately, super-grandmother-angel-woman was at it again. She jumped up yelling, "I'll look for it!" and ran out of the bus... into the rain... with no umbrella. "Which car is yours?" she yelled as she shielded her eyes from the raindrops. I pointed, speechless, and watched as she weaved in and around the other cars, searching between them and under them for the lost shoe. "It must still be inside," she concluded and got back on the bus. "Go check real quick," she said with the authority of a grandmother telling her granddaughter to wash up before supper. And seeing as how she had already pulled one-shoed Canaan into her wet lap, that's exactly what I did.

I found his shoe still in his car seat where she said it would be, and the rest of the morning was surprisingly uneventful. Somewhere along the way, I think I told the woman thank you, but I'm not even sure of that. I just know that after my boys were in their classrooms and I was walking alone to my Bible study class, I realized that my perfect picture of what I wanted my life to look like had changed that day.

I didn't want to stroll into church looking perfect and unflawed. Instead I wanted to be the church, the very body of Christ, with my hands and arms reaching out to help those around me just like this sweet lady had helped me. Without even knowing it, she taught me three tips for serving those in need.

First, she let her experience complement her service. Clearly, this woman had juggled her own children and baggage somewhere down the road and knew how valuable an extra set of hands can be to a mom with young kids.

Next, she saw a need and acted upon it. I love that this woman never asked me if I needed or wanted help. Instead, she just acted.

Finally, she went the extra mile. The woman literally ran into the rain for me. It would have been enough that she helped with my children and with my bags. But she didn't stop and she didn't let her own level of comfort dictate the amount of help she was willing to give.

God gives us our own experiences and our own trials for a reason. One of those reasons is to instill empathy in our lives that we may reach and help others who are going through similar trials. What about you? Do you seek opportunities to minister to others based on the trials you've experienced yourself? Do you see a need and act upon it immediately? Do you go the extra mile?

Sometimes it means simply sharing your umbrella. And other times it means running out in the rain, getting drenched, and showing the world what a "picture-perfect" Sunday morning *really* looks like.

In Thought

"Dear God, forget the super-Christian image; You can keep it. Forget the magazine-cover look of a perfect family; it's not important to me after all. Forget the untarnished, unused, ineffective shadow of a person, and instead, make me look like a servant! Amen."

In Word

- *Praise be to the God and Father of our Lord Jesus Christ, the Father of compassion and the God of all comfort, who comforts us in all our troubles, so that we can comfort those in any trouble with the comfort we ourselves have received from God.* 2 Corinthians 1:3-4 NIV
- *If someone forces you to go one mile, go with him two miles.* Matthew 5:41 NIV

In Deed

What are your three biggest trials you've experienced over the past few years? How could you use those experiences to help someone else?

Emily Ryan

21

God Loves a
Fearful Giver?

There is no fear in love. But perfect love casts out fear...
1 John 4:18a NIV

Several years ago, my family had a "Garage Giveaway." Not a garage "sale," but a "sale" where EVERYTHING WAS FREE!

We live in a world where it's often said that nothing is free.

This kind of mistrust of true giving was evidenced on the faces of some of our patrons that day during our garage giveaway. I remember a large family pulling up in a truck. A very young lady got out and was pretty far along in her pregnancy. Thankfully, I had a lot of baby things and maternity clothes to give away that day.

She looked at me with disbelief, as did the others, when I told her what she wanted to buy was FREE! I actually had to repeat it several times. As it began to sink in, their faces changed...sweet expressions replaced confused ones. Smiles broke out all around as they realized there was no "catch."

Oh, how fun that day was! It was exciting to watch others receive! We didn't even care about being thanked verbally; we could see the gratitude in their faces   .

In my younger years, I told the Lord at one time that I was going to quit tithing for a while to get out of debt. Well, the laugh was on me. After about three months of unfaithfulness in my giving back to the Lord what He owns, my finances were worse. Not only was I still in debt, but I then owed the Lord about $900 according to my earthly income. My actual debt to Him, of course, includes all that I have and all that I am.

Every time I've ever given, it has blessed me. The Lord, who "loves a cheerful giver," (2 Corinthians 9:7 NKJV) has blessed me. I don't mean this as "prosperity" teaching; however, the Lord has always provided for my needs and always blesses me in many ways when I give.

Now, going back to the world's mantra of "nothing is free." Hmmm... REALLY?

Grace – Salvation – Redemption? Those were bought not with anything I've ever paid, but with the blood of an innocent man on a cruel cross.

But the world does not understand this kind of giving. There must be a catch to it. How much do I have to pay to the church? How many "Hail Mary's" must I say? Maybe I just have to work my salvation out in the form of serving at the church or leading a ministry.

We must search our hearts to find and confess our fears about giving. It always comes down to a matter of trust. Whether it's giving money, giving time or giving talents, when we are resistant to giving, it's clear that we are focusing a whole lot on ourselves and very little on our Savior.

After all, He owns "the cattle on a thousand hills," (Psalm 50:10) and He owns us, too. Are we not grateful enough for the gift of His son not to cheerfully give ourselves back to Him?

Present your "fleece" before the Lord (see Judges 6:36-40) by giving back to Him what He already owns. Whether it is financial, serving, time, belongings or your prayer time, start giving on a regular basis, and then watch how the Lord will bless your life!

In Thought

"Dear Lord, I want to give cheerfully. Please take away all fear from my heart regarding giving to You. I know that "perfect love casts out fear." Help me to love You more deeply. Please show me how You want me to give, and then give me an excited desire to obey You in this. Thank You for all the ways in which You take care of me and my needs. Amen."

In Word

- *He who has a generous eye will be blessed, for he gives of his bread to the poor.* Proverbs 22:9 NKJV
- *The generous soul will be made rich, and he who waters will also be watered himself.* Proverbs 11:25 NKJV
- *I, the LORD, search the heart, I test the mind, even to give every man according to his ways, according to the fruit of his doings.* Jeremiah 17:10 NKJV

In Deed

- Go through your home, praying that the Lord will reveal what you need to give away and to whom you should give it.
- Pray over your finances, asking the Lord how much He wants you to give back to your church and various ministries, as well as to any individuals.
- Make a "gratitude" list of all the Lord has given you. Include *all* of your blessings, not just physical ones.

Kim Lindquist

Week 3 Notes

22
Putting Feet
to the Feat

However, I consider my life worth nothing to me, if only I may finish the race and complete the task the Lord Jesus has given me—the task of testifying to the gospel of God's grace.
Acts 20:24 NIV

To say that I am not a runner would be a huge understatement. Nevertheless, I still had a goal to someday run the whole three miles around Memorial Park in Houston without stopping.

My friend assured me that once you're comfortable running two miles, running more is not difficult, so when I was at the two-mile level, I decided to put my feet to the feat. I got up on a Saturday morning, donned my running shoes and sweats, and took off from a random starting point in the park. In no time at all, I rounded the first corner, but by the second corner, the outlook was not looking very good. It suddenly hit me that I had no clue how far I'd run or how far I had to go. The mile markers along the side of the path meant nothing to me because my starting point had been chosen at random. So for every yard I ran, I felt as if a mile of untraveled path added itself to the horizon. Frustrated and dejected, I finally quit running. As my friend continued without me, I realized how important it was for me to be familiar with my surroundings, have recognizable milestones, and maintain an expectant attitude.

But because I familiarized myself with the course during my walk of shame back to the car, the very next weekend I was able to run the whole way! Because I knew the path and recognized landmarks, I was able to measure my distance along the way. And because I had seen a friend accomplish the task with such ease the week before, I suddenly had an expectant attitude that I could do the same. I knew it wasn't as impressive as running a marathon or competing in a triathlon, but for me the three-mile accomplishment called for celebratory cartwheels.

In the New Testament, the Christian life is often referred to as a race, yet so many times we set out to complete the course the Lord has placed in front of us with the same kind of flippancy I had about my first attempt to run the park. We don't survey the big picture. We fail to set up recognizable goals, and we are often apathetic about our efforts at best.

We reach for intangible things like the fruit of the spirit (love, joy, peace, patience, kindness, goodness, faithfulness, gentleness and self-control, Galatians 5:22-23 NIV) but fail to convert those aspirations into measurable goals. We reach for peace, but neglect to walk away from a situation or person that causes turmoil. We want to become kind, but fail to translate that into everyday menial tasks. We aspire to have self-control, then wonder why we can't stop reaching for the thing we've neglected to put out of sight.

Sometimes even measurable goals go unmet because we fail to formulate recognizable milestones along the way. We want to read the Bible, but we don't break that down into a daily reading schedule. We want to see our loved ones come to accept Christ, but we don't pray for them on a regular basis. We want to tithe faithfully to the church, but we don't factor that into our monthly budget when we buy a new house.

We should approach our spiritual growth with no less thought or consideration than we do our career goals, our weight-loss goals, or our goals for saving for retirement. "Do you not know that in a race all the runners run, but only one gets the prize? Run in such a way as to get the prize" (1 Corinthians 9:24 NIV). In the end, it will lead to a celebration that calls for even more than cartwheels!

In Thought

"Dear Lord, open my eyes to the spiritual goals You wish for me to accomplish. Convict me of the areas of obedience that I am approaching only half-heartedly. You've already blessed me with a course that guarantees victory at the finish line; help me to run that course at a steady pace of faithfulness. Amen."

In Word

- *You have made known to me the path of life; you will fill me with joy in your presence, with eternal pleasures at your right hand.* Psalm 16:11 NIV
- *I have fought the good fight, I have finished the race, I have kept the faith.* 2 Timothy 4:7 NIV
- *Therefore, since we are surrounded by such a great cloud of witnesses, let us throw off everything that hinders and the sin that so easily entangles, and let us run with perseverance the race marked out for us. Let us fix our eyes on Jesus, the author and perfecter of our faith, who for the joy set before him endured the cross, scorning its shame, and sat down at the right hand of the throne of God.* Hebrews 12:1-2 NIV

In Deed

- Name one or two specific goals you have in your spiritual life.
- Now, formulate a plan to complete those goals. If it's reading the Bible, determine how many pages/verses/chapters you need to read daily in order to accomplish the task. If it's praying, schedule 30-minute "meetings" on your calendar and spend that time in prayer. If it's witnessing, name three people you want to share Christ with and invite them to next Sunday's service at your church.

Emily Ryan

23

Who's in Your Family Tree?

In everything we do, we show that we are true ministers of God. We patiently endure troubles and hardships and calamities of every kind.
2 Corinthians 6:4 NLT

When I hit 40, I got a sudden urge to trace the lineage of my family, particularly my father's side. As a little girl, I was enthralled by the stories of his childhood. His mother was married at 15 and gave birth to seven children before her first husband died of tuberculosis. Two years later, she married a childless 54-year-old widower and gave birth to my father in September of 1921. He was to be their only offspring because she and a baby died in childbirth three years later.

When his father died of a heart attack in 1924, the seven older half siblings were doled out to live with various relatives. My dad was placed in a Salvation Army orphanage in Greenville, South Carolina. Safely surrounded by both parents in a home that lacked little in the way of comfort, I was saddened that such profound tragedy would be the hallmark of my father's young life.

Years later, I dove deeply into the gene pool of my past in regular visits to the Clayton Library Center for Genealogical Research. There I diligently searched census records for my ancestors and even discovered a book recounting the wounding and subsequent death of my great grandfather in the Civil War. It was exciting and I loved sharing my information with my dad. But the most important information came via the internet when I discovered a relative who had already traced our family back to William Hudson born in London in 1541. He had done all the work for us and even sent a book to us detailing each generation up to the present.

What had seemed an impossible task had been completed quickly and with little effort. But as I perused the pages and pages of names I realized it wasn't just the lineage that had so intrigued me; it was the stories behind the names. My ancestors were people with incredible resiliency and admirable character who braved a vast ocean to settle a new land. Scratching out a living from the rocky soil, facing sickness and hardship, they refused to be defeated by life's sorrows. Looking back I could see their storyline was one of God's unfailing faithfulness.

Though he had lost his biological parents, in the orphanage my father was taught the truths of the Bible by godly caretakers who loved him and trained him to be studious and hardworking. Eventually he became an Air Force pilot and later an engineer who designed systems for the first manned flights into space - quite an achievement for an orphan from the Carolina Piedmont. What I had viewed as tragic events were the very things God used to spur him on to great accomplishments.

Each one of us faces opposition in some form throughout our lives. It may be a chronic illness, an errant child, a wayward spouse, loss of employment, or even the death of a loved one. The question is, how will we respond? We can become bitter and blame subsequent poor choices on our misfortune, or we can acknowledge the fact that God had allowed such difficulties to make us into inspiring characters in the unique story He is creating for our descendants.

In Thought

"Heavenly Father, I acknowledge You as the author of my story. I believe that nothing touches me except that which should cause me to seek You with all my heart. Thank You for Your Word where I find hope and encouragement through the stories of my ancestors in the faith. Amen."

In Word

- *We can rejoice, too, when we run into problems and trials, for we know that they help us develop endurance. And endurance develops strength of character, and character strengthens our confident hope of salvation.* Romans 5:3-4 NLT
- *So humble yourselves under the mighty power of God, and at the right time he will lift you up in honor. Give all your worries and cares to God for he cares about you.* 1 Peter 5:6, 7 NLT

In Deed

- Read the life story of Joseph in Genesis 30-50. What setbacks and disappointments did Joseph face in his life? How did God use those things for His glory?
- List the disappointments and setbacks in your own life. Now pray that God would supernaturally work all of those things together for good.

Janie Southard

89

24
Why Not Me?

---

*"Therefore, if anyone is in Christ, he is a new creation;
the old has gone, the new is here!"*
2 Corinthians 5:17 NIV

Years ago, I was struck with a life-changing work injury. Suddenly, I was without my health, my job, and I had little support from those around me. I was filled with anger, pain and despair about my situation, but I kept praying. My favorite question was, "Why me, Lord?" What I didn't realize at the time was that I should have been asking, "Why not me, Lord?" Many times in our lives, we are faced with situations like Paul's Damascus road experience, requiring that we change our thinking about who we are, where we are going and what we are doing. These detours challenge us in a myriad of ways, often forcing us to look at everything we think we know and reevaluate our thinking process.

My experience called for me to examine my overly self-reliant attitude. I was leaning too much on myself. I was a Christian, but God was not at the center of my life. I prayed, but didn't wait or allow God to work before trying to fix things myself. Now, I had nothing to fall back on. Like Paul, I had to trust God completely for the first time in my life! I had to follow without sight where He led. It was truly an enlightening experience for me as I struggled to put God back into the center of my life and allow everything to revolve around Him.

I love the story of the apostle Paul. I became fascinated by the story of this man who transformed his life so dramatically for his God. Paul, initially a Pharisee, was a persecutor of the church. He was there when Stephen, the first martyr, was stoned to death, giving sanction to his murder. Then Paul encountered Jesus on the road to Damascus! Struck blind for three days, he surely had ample time to think about his life. However, Paul did what many of us do not. He changed. He left behind everything he knew about himself and everything he thought he knew about God in order to really get to know Him.

We cannot live our lives without change. Jesus Christ came to change the world. He called His disciples to leave the safety and comfort of their everyday lives, attitudes and opinions to follow Him in a world where others would ultimately kill them for their beliefs! But these men shed every prior belief in order to do so. Can we do less?

What is God asking you to do today? Perhaps it is to forgive someone who has hurt you, to step out in faith with a decision about your life, finances or family matters, or to serve in some capacity in the church. Whatever it is, the first step is prayer. Pray for the guidance of the Holy Spirit. Then, once you have God's answer, act on it! Don't allow doubt to hinder you from applying what God is telling you to do.

In Thought

"Dear God, may my eyes and heart be truly open today for all the opportunities You will present for me to grow and change to follow Your sovereign will. Help me, like Paul, to meet every challenge with willingness, faith and trust in You. Amen."

In Word

Then Job replied to the Lord: "I know that you can do anything, and no one can stop you. You asked, 'Who is this that questions my wisdom with such ignorance?' It is I—and I was talking about things I knew nothing about, things far too wonderful for me. You said, 'Listen and I will speak! I have some questions for you, and you must answer them.' I had only heard about you before, but now I have seen you with my own eyes. I take back everything I said, and I sit in dust and ashes to show my repentance." Job 42:1-6 NLT

In Deed

- Is there a situation in your life right now that has you asking, "Why me, Lord?" If so, spend some time in prayer sincerely asking Him, "Why not me, Lord?"
- Make a list of three things you can do to change and conform to His will. Now do those things today.

Patricia Dixon

25
American Idols

You shall have no other gods before Me.
Exodus 20:3 NKJV

As my friend and I drove up to the theater that day in 1978, I saw that the line for the movie we'd been waiting for stretched from the ticket booth all the way past the end of the building. We quickly walked to get in line. Then, it began to rain. I have to say, in all my years of movie going, this was a first. I stood in the rain for 30 minutes to see Warren Beatty up close and personal (from the front row) in *Heaven Can Wait*. We felt one could never be too close to that face, and the wait was worth it!

Throughout my years, there has never been any other time I waited in the rain to see the latest heart throb in America, but there were many other attempts to catch a glimpse of the stars. I remember driving around during my lunch hour to try to find Sam Elliot in Kemah (where his movie was being filmed), waiting outside the Astrodome after a game to see the cutest player on the team, putting up numerous David Cassidy posters in my room as a young girl and going to see him in concert wearing a T-shirt that read, "Manilow Maniac."

As I matured, some of those stars were, of course, no longer obsessions for me. But there were other, more realistic things that stole my attention to an extreme degree. These real-life "idols" included the man I married, his children, our son, friends, the works I did at church, the works I did outside of church, and a few hobbies. Of course, there was also perhaps the most insidious idol of them all: *my time.* Although all of these things are blessings from the Lord and are not necessarily evil in and of themselves, they all have the potential to take more of our time, our thoughts, and our energy than we give to the Lord Jesus Christ.

Noah Webster's 1828 dictionary defines an idol as, "Anything on which we set our affections; that to which we indulge an excessive and sinful attachment." Webster adds, "An idol is any thing which usurps the place of God in the hearts of His rational creatures."

Anything, indeed, can become an idol! Are we spending more time on Facebook than we are seeking His face through His book? Are we having a relationship with our iPhone rather than with the great I Am? Does our "social network" require electricity rather than face-to-face encounters with those God wants for His kingdom?

It's all in whom or what we worship. It's okay to admire a musician, an author, an actor or technology. It's expected that we love our families and our friends with the love of Jesus. And it's true that faith without works is dead (James 2:17). The sin happens when we love things or people more than we love our Lord. He will not share His throne in any way. He is, indeed, above all and over all. He is to be the very air we breathe and is the only person to be worshipped. Pursue Him, run after holiness, and become obsessed with loving Him!

In Thought

"Dear Lord, please show me anyone or anything in my life that I've placed higher than You. Take away any pride I have in my works, and remind me that all of "my" time is actually Your time. Please destroy my worship of any other "gods" and restore those things to their proper position beneath the cross. Amen."

In Word

- *Flee also youthful lusts; but pursue righteousness, faith, love, peace with those who call on the Lord out of a pure heart.* 2 Timothy 2:22 NKJV
- *For the weapons of our warfare are not carnal, but mighty through God to the pulling down of strong holds; casting down imaginations, and every high thing that exalteth itself against the knowledge of God, and bringing into captivity every thought to the obedience of Christ.* 2 Corinthians 10:4-5 KJV
- *All nations whom You have made shall come and worship before You, O Lord, and shall glorify Your name. For You are great, and do wondrous things; You alone are God.* Psalm 86:9-10 NKJV

In Deed

Spend time alone with the Lord asking Him to reveal what or whom you are "worshipping" other than Him. Make a list of these and then commit them all back to the Lord. Ask Him to forgive you and commit to spending at least 15 minutes each day this week alone with Him in prayer with no distractions.

Kim Lindquist

26
Demolition Derby

---

*Walk in all the way that the LORD your God has
commanded you, so that you may live and prosper and
prolong your days in the land that you will possess.*
Deuteronomy 5:33 NIV

I usually don't make New Year's resolutions because as soon as I don't follow through with one, I get depressed and negative thoughts start to seep in. However, this year I did make a couple of resolutions, and so far I've stuck with them. I resolved to get healthy and fit and strengthen my walk with God. The funny part is that the hardest challenge of those for me has been the getting fit part; I love to eat.

Some time ago I was headed down a path of destruction even though I was involved in church. I began seeking peace from alcohol and relieving my stresses of family life at the bar. I was miserable even though, temporarily, it felt good. I knew that living that way would not promise me a long future with my children, but it was still hard to turn my life around.

Finally, I hit rock bottom during a family member's wedding in Galveston. Even though I was there with my children, I still proceeded to drink myself into a stupor. I made a complete fool of myself by the end of the night, and my twelve-year-old daughter said something to me about it the next day. I was ashamed when I realized what I'd done. I said, "No more!" and asked God for grace and forgiveness. I wanted to obey God's commands, not just read about them.

I began having quiet times with Him in the morning, faithfully reading His Word and choosing to obey it. I told Him I was tired of my sinful ways and wanted to get close to Him. God desires us not only to accept Him as Lord over our life; but also to obey His commands. We are to spend time with Him, treat others with love and respect, stay in His Word and live out the teachings of Christ to those around us.

God's love for me immediately gave me peace and let me know that change is possible when we set our hearts on Him. Have I prospered? Oh yes; I'm at home spending more time with my children and instilling in them God's love and design for our lives.

In Thought

"Oh Father, I pray that I would continually seek Your face and Your Word to lead me every day. I pray I would always obey Your truths and instructions for my life and never turn away from Your love and grace. Thank You for second chances and for continually blessing my life. Amen."

In Word

- *Whatever you do, work at it with all your heart, as working for the Lord, not for men.* Colossians 3:23 NIV
- *Flee from all this, and pursue righteousness, godliness, faith, love, endurance and gentleness. Fight the good fight of the faith. Take hold of the eternal life to which you were called when you made your good confession in the presence of many*

witnesses. 1Timothy 6:11-12 NIV
- *Be very careful, then, how you live-not as unwise but as wise.* Ephesians 5:15 NIV

In Deed
- What is it that God is convicting you to give up? Alcohol? Gossip? Television? Develop an "escape route" to follow whenever you face temptation in that area.
- Share your resolution for change with a trusted friend, and together pray that God will strengthen you daily as you flee temptation.

Cindy Cañas

27
Gagged and Dragged

But each one is tempted when, by his own evil desire, he is dragged away and enticed.
James 1:14 NIV

It was almost midnight on a Friday night, and I was returning home from a church social with a friend. We were stopped at a stoplight just a block away from home and didn't even notice the black BMW in front of us. That is, we didn't notice it until the trunk slowly opened and a boy, clad only in duct tape and blue boxer shorts, climbed out of it.

His hands were bound, his mouth was taped shut, and his eyes were wide with fear. He took a split second to survey his surroundings and then dashed across oncoming traffic racing towards a nearby neighborhood. Seconds later, two boys from inside the BMW flung open their doors and chased after him, one waving a baseball bat high over his head as he ran.

My heart started pounding, and I double-checked my doors to make sure they were locked. On impulse, I grabbed my cell phone and dialed 9-1-1. Since the trunk on the BMW was still open, I couldn't see the license plate number I wanted to report, so when the BMW sped through the light, I was hot on its tail, waiting for the trunk to shut with the acceleration. I yelled at the 9-1-1 operator the minute

I could see the plate, "Take down this license plate! Take down this number!" Then, figuring it unwise to continue following the car full of angry teenagers, I let them get away and parked on a side street to finish reporting the crime.

"Let's see if we can find the boy!" I said as I hung up the phone, and we drove around the neighborhood looking for any sign of the boy or the BMW. Finally, when we were stopped at the same stoplight as before, we saw the car again. Across the street in a restaurant parking lot, five police cars appeared as if from nowhere and surrounded the black BMW. The policemen got out, guns drawn, and slowly approached the car.

My friend and I watched from a distance as the scene unfolded. The cops lined the boys along the side of the BMW and slammed their hands on the hood. Then they opened the trunk of the car revealing the same half-naked, scared little boy inside. They helped him out of the trunk as my friend and I bounced up and down in victory celebrating that the boy was finally safe, and that we had been instrumental in his release.

When Christians are in sin, we should be like that boy locked in the trunk. That boy had to be forced into the trunk. He had to be bound, gagged and dragged into captivity before the hood of the trunk slammed down on top of him. And once inside, he didn't give up and accept defeat. Instead, as soon as the first opportunity to escape presented itself, he took off running as far and as fast as he could away from his captors.

The Bible says that "each one is tempted when, by his own evil desire, he is dragged away and enticed" (James 1:14 NIV). James thought highly of us when he said that we had to be "dragged away and enticed" into sin. Many times that's not the case at all. All too often, all Satan has to do is *suggest* we get in the trunk and we hop in voluntarily and close the hood for him.

We should approach the possibility of falling into temptation with the same drive and determination we would use if someone was trying to lock us into the trunk of a car. We should fight it! We should run from it! And at the very first chance, we should escape it!

In Thought

"Dear Lord, please forgive me for all the times that I've fallen into sin without a fight and for the times when a chance to escape presents itself but I foolishly ignore the conviction. I pray that I would not find comfort in the dark damp trunk of sin, but that I would turn to You, who conquered sin on the cross, for my strength and my freedom. Amen."

In Word

- *No temptation has seized you except what is common to man. And God is faithful; he will not let you be tempted beyond what you can bear. But when you are tempted, he will also provide a way out so that you can stand up under it.* 1 Corinthians 10:13 NIV
- *For we do not have a high priest who is unable to sympathize with our weaknesses, but we have one who has been tempted in every way, just as we are--yet was without sin.* Hebrews 4:15 NIV

In Deed

- The first step in avoiding sin is knowing where you are weak. Take some time to evaluate your weaknesses and write down three areas of your life in which you are more likely to fall for

Satan's suggestions rather than fight off his efforts.

- Find a trusted friend and ask that person to hold you accountable in those three areas.
- Spend some time formulating an "escape plan" from those temptations ahead of time. Since God promises that He will always provide a way out when we are tempted, it's often easier to resist temptation when we have thought ahead of time about how we can escape it.

Emily Ryan

28

The Blessings Book

I will give thanks to you, LORD, with all my heart; I will tell of all your wonderful deeds. I will be glad and rejoice in you; I will sing the praises of your name, O Most High.
Psalm 9:1-2 NIV

Since I can remember, I have been writing "thank you" notes. I wish I could say this was always my idea and that I was born with an innately grateful heart, but I have to give full credit to my mother for instilling this valuable skill in me. Growing up, I remember being resentful that my toy or money was being held hostage until I produced a sincere letter of thankfulness to the giver. I was probably the youngest person to learn how to spell sincerely correctly. It is funny, now that I look back on it, that I would produce these angelic little cards while my heart was fuming, but my mom never wavered. My brother and I were taught to show our appreciation to those who did something for us through a little note that took only a minute to write. I did not realize how those acts of being grateful would impact my life until I was an adult.

When my fiancé and I began planning our wedding, we compiled our guest list. It was fun at first, but it translated to months of long hours of work. I will never forget my mom reminding me that there would be some gifts, and of course, I would need to thank every person for each present. She offered to address and stamp the envelopes for me, and that was when the Blessings Book came about. We numbered each line, followed by the giver's name and the description of the gift as they were opened. My mom then went through the list of names and addressed the envelopes. She would then pass the stack off to me with the Blessings Book. I went back through the book, wrote the thank you note and then highlight the line when the envelope was sealed and ready to be mailed. I will never forget my mom keeping me accountable and tracking my progress each day as she would thumb through the pages. The day came, a few weeks after the wedding, that the last card was mailed! I was very excited when I gave the Blessings Book back to my mom and went on with my life.

Two years later, we were expecting our first child and were so excited. It was during all the elation that mom approached me with the Blessings Book in hand. She said with a smile, "Don't forget to thank those who give you gifts for the new baby." I knew the work ahead, but I understood the importance of showing my gratitude. A few pages later we had thanked everyone who had taken the time to give us a gift for the baby and welcomed our first born son into the world. This time I did not return the book; instead, I asked if I could keep it. My mom smiled and said, "I am so proud of you!"

From that moment on, any gift that comes to us is recorded in the Blessings Book and a thank you note is promptly sent. I know my boys will probably be upset with me just like I was with my mom when they do not get to have their gift until a little note of gratitude is written. And now, each time we pull the book out for a gift giving occasion, I love to thumb through the highlighted pages and remember the friends who took the time to bless me and my family!

So many times we teach our children the importance of giving to others, but sometimes forget to teach them how to be a grateful recipient of gifts. Stopping to thank someone for a gift or a helpful service can be a very humbling experience because you have to actually stop your life to be grateful. As Christians, we have received the ultimate gift of salvation from Jesus Christ who died on the cross. Can you imagine accepting this gift without thanking the One who died so we could have it? Just like the story in Luke 17 when Jesus healed the ten lepers and only one came back to thank Him…take time to thank your Savior today!

In Thought
"Lord, thank You for saving me from my sins. Thank You for loving me so much that You died for my undeserving heart. I love You. Teach me to be grateful for all the provisions that I have been given. Amen."

In Word
One of them, when he saw he was healed, came back, praising God in a loud voice. He threw himself at Jesus' feet and thanked him—and he was a Samaritan. Jesus asked, "Were not all ten cleansed? Where are the other nine? Has no one returned to give praise to God except this foreigner?" Then he said to him, "Rise and go; your faith has made you well." Luke 17:15-19 NIV

In Deed
- Write a thank you note to Jesus for being your Savior and keep it where you can be reminded of His great love for you.
- Start a Blessings Book of your own. Record every gift you receive and promptly thank each giver. Make sure he or she knows how grateful you are for their blessings.

Mikelle Challenger

Week 4 Notes

_____

_____

_____

_____

_____

_____

_____

_____

_____

_____

_____

_____

_____

_____

_____

_____

29
Gardening
of the Heart

---

*Still other seeds fell on fertile soil, and they sprouted,
grew, and produced a crop that was thirty, sixty, and
even a hundred times as much as had been planted.*
Mark 4:8 NLT

When I was visiting the sleepy little Alabama town of my mother's birth, my Aunt Ida Mae gave me a tour of her garden. It sloped down one of the rolling hills beside her house and was alive with brilliant colors. Overhead tall pines swayed in the breeze. Their falling needles made soft pathways around the beds and with each crunchy step the pungent fragrance of pine assailed my nostrils. I breathed deeply, savoring an unforgettable smell of my childhood as we walked. Standing tall was a deep orange flower curved so that it resembled a boiled shrimp. With her worn hands, my aunt stooped and gently lifted part of the root ball from the soft, loamy soil and wrapped it in damp newspaper ready for the trip back to Houston. When I arrived home, tired from traveling 500 miles with a baby and a toddler, I haphazardly dug a hole and mounded the Texas earth around it. Despite my lack of attention, the shrimp plant thrived and has multiplied so that it threatens to overtake its neighbors and escape the confines of the stone border. Now, over 15 years later, it sways gently over the claw foot tub in the garden that is home to our goldfish.

Throughout my childhood, my Aunt Ida Mae offered a safe haven amid what was often a stormy life of uncertainty. My dad was in the military so we moved almost every year. My mother hovered precariously between depression and unexplained gaiety due to alcoholism. Though we sometimes went to church, God was not a part of our everyday lives, but with my aunt, I felt secure and saw a daily dependency on the Lord that was not lived out in our home. I blossomed just as her plants, basking in the warmth of Aunt Ida Mae's praise and encouragement.

Often summer visits coincided with Vacation Bible School at the little Baptist church she attended. Though she worked full time, Aunt Ida Mae was never too busy to take me there. In that simple, white, clapboard building on the outskirts of town, I marched to "Onward Christian Soldiers" and drank red Kool-Aid and ate homemade cookies, satisfying my soul and my stomach. At the time I had no idea that my aunt's actions were evidence of her true gardening skills. During those oppressive south Alabama summers, she saw to it that the seeds of faith were deeply planted in my young heart. Years later they produced a harvest of righteousness when at 27 I trusted the Lord Jesus Christ as my Savior.

Remembering Aunt Ida Mae and how she coaxed such a dazzling display of color from the earth magnifies my satisfaction as I plunge my fingers into the dark, rich soil each spring. Like hers, my garden thrives and is lush and green even in the sweltering heat of a Houston summer. But my most cherished heritage from this dear lady is the example of a life lived tirelessly serving the Lord by planting and watering seeds of faith in young hearts. From Aunt Ida Mae I learned that, without a doubt, it is the most important gardening I will ever do. However, sometimes we don't want to be needed; life is so much easier if we have to care only for ourselves. Investing in the lives of others, especially children, often takes time and energy we don't want to give. But that is not the example that Jesus set for us. Instead, He met one need after another for anyone who asked of Him, especially children. Finally, He met the greatest need of all: the sacrifice of His life for ours as He hung battered and bleeding on a cross.

In Thought

"How grateful I am to You, Lord, for giving Your life for me. I thank You that You placed caring people in my life to show Your love and mercy and led me into a relationship with You. I pray that I will never miss an opportunity to sow and water the seeds of faith in the lives of others, even if it means getting on my knees and digging into some dirt. Please show me each day the ways that I can serve You by encouraging others to become firmly rooted in Your Word. Amen."

In Word

- *Jesus replied, "The Son of Man is the farmer who plants the good seed. The field is the world, and the good seed represents the people of the Kingdom."* Matthew 13:37 NLT
- *Anyone who welcomes a little child like this on my behalf welcomes me, and anyone who welcomes me welcomes not only me but also my Father who sent me.* Mark 9:37 NLT
- *For you have been born again, but not to a life that will quickly end. Your new life will last forever because it comes from the eternal, living word of God. As the Scriptures say, "People are like grass; their beauty is like a flower in the field. The grass withers and the flower fades. But the word of the Lord remains forever." And that word is the Good News that was preached to you.* 1 Peter 1:23-25 NLT

In Deed

When you hear that workers are needed to minister to children or youth, prayerfully consider if God wants to use you to sow and water seeds of faith in the fertile soil of young hearts. Even if your children are grown or you've never had children, God tells us that they are some of the most precious ones in His kingdom.

Janie Southard

30

Are You Under?

"Can anyone hide in secret places so that I cannot see him?" declares the Lord.
Jeremiah 23:24a NIV

One of my favorite childhood games was one my father made up that we called "Are you under?" He'd cup his large hands together and place his pinkies on my forehead and his thumbs on his, bridging our eyes together under a tunnel of darkness. The darkness created a cave of refuge that I willingly entered, and though only my eyes were covered, I curled up into a ball as if my entire body was hidden from view. That's when he'd whisper, "Are you under?" I'd nod my head excitedly, foolishly believing that because I could not see anyone else, others could not see me either.

And so it was for years; I'd cover my eyes and think I was safely hidden, not realizing that being "under" didn't hide me at all. But even after time and wisdom taught me otherwise, I still watched as my dad played "Are you under?" with other kids – my siblings, my nieces, and finally, my own children – and saw that each one reacted the same way I had. Once their eyes were covered, they'd curl up into a ball and begin to whisper as if they were completely hidden from the outside world.

"Can anyone hide in secret places so that I cannot see him?" declares the Lord, (Jeremiah 23:24a). There are many times when we, in our Christian walks, cover our eyes in an effort to hide from God. Perhaps we are ashamed of sin, so we quit looking at Him, and somehow believe that because we cannot see God, He cannot see us either. But He can.

Maybe we quit going to church because we think we won't run into God anywhere else. We quit reading our Bibles because we think that will silence Him. We bury ourselves under a tunnel of apathy, and stay there so long that we come to believe that God has forgotten about us because He can no longer see us. But the reality is that it is *we* who can no longer see *Him* anymore, not the other way around.

Are you under? If so, realize that God can still see you. You are not hidden. You are not forgotten. You are not neglected. You are simply under.

In Thought

"Dear Lord, thank You that You can see me. Thank You that even when my eyes are closed and I cannot see You, You are still watching. You see my actions. You see my thoughts. You see my motives. I pray that I would not try to hide from You because hide, I cannot. Reveal to me the areas of my life about which I have kept silent, and help me speak about them openly to You, realizing that You know and You can see every last detail already. Amen."

In Word

*   *Where can I go from your Spirit? Where can I flee from your presence? If I go up to the heavens, you are there; if I make my bed in the depths, you are there. If I rise on the wings of the dawn, if I settle on the far side of the sea, even there your hand*

will guide me, your right hand will hold me fast. If I say, "Surely the darkness will hide me and the light become night around me," even the darkness will not be dark to you; the night will shine like the day, for darkness is as light to you. Psalm 139:7-12 NIV

• *"Am I only a God nearby," declares the Lord, "and not a God far away? Can anyone hide in secret places so that I cannot see him?" declares the Lord. "Do not I fill heaven and earth?" declares the Lord. Jeremiah 23:23-24 NIV*

In Deed

• Spend some time outdoors praying with your eyes open. Look around at nature and realize how big God is.
• Now close your eyes as you continue to pray and think about how, though you can no longer see God in the nature that surrounds you, He can still see you.
• Finally, praise Him that though He is big enough to have created you and all that surrounds you, He's still small enough to know you intimately.

Emily Ryan

31
The Money Pit

*Those who hope in the LORD will renew their strength.
They will soar on wings like eagles; they will run and not
grow weary, they will walk and not be faint.*
Isaiah 40:31 NIV

Have you ever been in the wilderness? Not the one where you pitch a tent and roast marshmallows, but the true wilderness called life. My family and I have been in the wilderness for six months now, and hope is our only way of making it. At the end of June 2010, my husband was called into his supervisor's office about thirty minutes before it was time to go for the evening. They informed him that someone had to go and his name was drawn out of the hat. Wow – talk about a shock. My husband called me to let me know he had to turn in his phone and briefly shared what had happened. When I got off the phone, I had a strange mixture of emotions ranging from fear to peace. I cried for about thirty minutes also called my good friend and spiritual mother, Mary Palmer. She gave me some encouraging words and not too long after getting off the phone with her, I had a sense of peace. The Holy Spirit told me everything was going to be okay. Since then we have had to totally rely on God for our finances and for our strength to get from one month to the next. We have four children and our main concern is to keep our burdens from them and protect their innocence.

God has provided for us through our church family as well as our own families, and He has given us that last breath sometimes when our wings were drooping. When we think nothing more could happen to us and it does, He continues to say, "Trust me." With each rejection my husband has had to rely on God's strength and encouragement not to beat himself up with insecurity. We don't know how long we will remain in this particular wilderness, but we will continue to seek God's strength so that we don't become weary. Through Christ we can soar forever!

In Thought

"Heavenly Father, thank You so much for Your faithfulness and for Your renewed strength as we go day by day through this wilderness called life. I pray for those who are suffering right now and wondering how they will make it to tomorrow. Lord, just give us a little more wind beneath our wings to sustain us until Your will is completed in this phase of our lives; give us the peace we need to feel like the eagle soaring in the sky among the heavenly clouds. Great is Thy faithfulness! Amen."

In Word

- *This I call to mind and therefore I have hope: Because of the LORD's great love we are not consumed, for his compassions never fail.* Lamentations 3:21-22 NIV
- *Hope does not disappoint us, because God has poured out his love into our hearts by the Holy Spirit, whom he has given us.* Romans 5:5 NIV
- *The LORD is good to those whose hope is in him, to the one who seeks him; it is good to wait quietly for the salvation of the LORD.* Lamentations 3:25-26 NIV

In Deed

- If you are going through a trying time, start reading the book of James.
- Pray to God openly and honestly about what you are going through and how you are feeling. Allow His strength to renew you and give you the peace and hope you need to make it through the wilderness.
- Consult a friend or church staff member who will give you godly wisdom and direction.

Cindy Cañas

32
There's No Place Like Home(s)

For we know that if the earthly tent we live in is destroyed, we have a building from God, an eternal house in heaven, not built by human hands.
2 Corinthians 5:1 NIV

My son, Garrett, loves to visit people in their homes! He is the epitome of a social being who never tires of traveling. It matters not the size of the house or the condition in which we find it. Cluttered, clean, brick, wood – they are all a delight. Of course, he loves people dearly too, so visiting homes where people live is the best of both worlds. And if they have dogs, well, he's just elated! He'll bring an old church directory to me, point to who he wants to visit, and bring me the phone to call and ask if we can visit. I literally called seven people one weekend looking for someone to go see. If you haven't received a call from us yet, just give us time and we'll probably get to you!

We've also had some pretty interesting talks trying to explain to our son exactly why he cannot visit Whoville or why we can't go to the homes of people in the obituaries. (He actually brought the obituary page over to my husband, pointed to the pictures of the deceased, and told us "house" in sign language!)

There are times, however, when our hobby is touring homes without residents – model homes. I tell the real estate agent that we are not seriously looking, that it is just our hobby, and every realtor in the Houston area has been more than hospitable to us. We were quite disappointed when the huge house my son picked out for us to live in (larger than we would ever need, of course) sold and we couldn't visit it anymore. But we pass the time between house visits by drawing pictures of homes and looking them up on the computer, thanks to Google Maps and Google Earth.

There are worse things to be obsessed with than houses, but can you imagine what excitement Garrett will have when he sees his *eternal* home one day? A home like he's never known with "many rooms" (John 14:2). And the best part? He will *never* have to leave! He won't even have a desire to leave!

How many times do we forget that this world is not our home? As a people saved by Jesus through His grace and mercy, we are all to be "roommates" in our eternal home of heaven.

Think for a moment of your favorite house you've lived in or your favorite room as a child. Neither compares to your home in heaven.

We will never have to adjust the thermostat, pay a water bill (we'll have Living Water), fix something to eat (we'll be in the presence of the Bread of Life), or mow the grass in Houston heat! Perhaps we'd be more patient with circumstances or with the people around us if we remembered we are just temporary residents here. In a sense, we're all just renting a room in this earthly house. It will get better.

Someone once said that we aren't to be "so heavenly minded that we're of no earthly good." I know that means we aren't to neglect our duties and responsibilities on this earth while we're here just because those things are temporary, but it seems we've gone too far in the opposite direction. At times, we are so focused on our earthly responsibilities, trials and treasures that we forget what lies ahead for us.

What a mighty hope we have in an amazing future with the Lord in His mansion!

In Thought
"Dear Lord, thank You that this earth is not all there is. I can't wait to be with You in Glory and live in the home You have prepared for me. Please reveal to me how to touch people with Your love here on earth as I anticipate living in a house built with Your love in the hereafter! Amen."

In Word
*   *Surely your goodness and love will follow me all the days of my life, and I will dwell in the house of the LORD forever.* Psalm 23:6 NIV
*   *They shall neither hunger anymore nor thirst anymore; the sun shall not strike them, nor any heat; for the Lamb who is in the midst of the throne will shepherd them and lead them to living fountains of waters. And God will wipe away every tear from their eyes.* Revelation 7:16-17 NKJV

In Deed
If you feel discouraged carrying out your earthly duties this week – such as paying bills, doing repairs, or just doing daily tedious tasks – stop and sing songs of praise aloud to the Lord. This will remind you of your real estate in heaven!

Kim Lindquist

33
Be Strong and Take Heart

---

*Wait for the Lord; be strong and take heart
and wait for the Lord.*
Psalm 27:14 NIV

Sometimes you find yourself in a situation where all you can do is fall on your face before the Lord and plead for His divine guidance. That is where Bob found himself a few years ago when a small group of us arrived as missionaries to a foreign country that is does not welcome the love of Jesus.

Bob had spent a restless night praying and wondering if maybe he should just take the team and return home. He had information that there were some security issues and that it may not be safe for us to remain in the country. He felt a great burden of responsibility for those of us on his team. It was a very long night for him, and in the morning he still was not sure what to do.

Our group was small – just three men and two women – and we were to all meet for breakfast in the morning. The men were already there when my roommate and I walked in. I do not remember exactly what I said, but it was something about it being a glorious day and that I was excited to see what God was going to do that day. Whatever the words were, Bob knew at that moment that the message was from God and that we were to stay and fulfill God's purpose at that time and place. He says he felt an immediate peace about staying.

So stay, we did, and at no time did any of us ever feel as if we were in any danger. In fact, to this day, that mission trip is one of the most memorable I have taken.

Many times we find ourselves in a situation similar to the one Bob was in. We are unsure if we should stay or go, and we don't know exactly how God is leading us. The best thing we can do in times like these is to pray and wait and listen. God hears our prayers. Sometimes His answers come in unusual ways. You have to be watching and listening.

In Thought
"Lord, thank You for providing the answers to our prayers. Thank You for the comfort You give even during the periods of waiting. Forgive me for being impatient, and help me to wait on You. Amen."

In Word
- *Now faith is being sure of what we hope for and certain of what we do not see.* Hebrews 11:1 NIV
- *I will instruct you and teach you in the way you should go; I will counsel you and watch over you.* Psalm 32:8 NIV
- *The Lord will keep you from all harm—he will watch over your life; the Lord will watch over your coming and going both now and forevermore.* Psalm 121:7-8 NIV

In Deed
- Use a concordance or an online Bible study tool to read about how God led the Israelites by a pillar of cloud by day and a pillar of fire by night.
- The next time you are uncertain about the direction you should take, pray that God would make His path for you just as clear.

Sharon Rigsby

34
Too Much Weight?

Don't worry about anything; instead, pray about everything. Tell God what you need, and thank Him for all He has done. Then you will experience God's peace, which exceeds anything we can understand. His peace will guard your hearts and minds as you live in Christ Jesus.
Philippians 4:6-7 NLT

Summertime. Time to get into the attic and get down the clothes that have been hibernating all winter long in their vacuum-sealed Space Bags. Those cute, white Capri's… what's this? A little tight. Did the dry cleaner shrink them at the end of last summer? Well, if he did, he shrank my yellow ones and my pink ones, too. This can't be. Back on the scale, one… no, two pounds more than last month. Pretty sure this totals five pounds more than this time last year. What's happening? Sure, I'm not 40-something anymore, but still. And I admit I did have a bit of fun at Thanksgiving, Christmas, New Year's Eve, Valentine's Day, my anniversary, my birthday, spring time picnics – well, the list goes on for a year! Guess the "weight" of my actions will continue until I purposefully do something about it.

Sometimes the problems of this world seem to surround and smother us, too. We feel heavy and the weight of the problems begins to make us lose hope. We begin to feel that we are sinking. Recently, I've experienced that – the heaviness of family problems was weighing me down. As I was listening to the radio during the Christmas season, Amy Grant's song "Breath of Heaven" was playing. That song tells of possible thoughts that were going on in Mary's head and heart as she carried Jesus in her womb. As I listened to the words, I began to sing them to the Lord from me.

I am waiting in a silent prayer
I am frightened by the load I bear.
In a world as cold as stone
Must I walk this path alone?
Be with me now. Be with me now.

Breath of Heaven, hold me together.
Be forever near me, Breath of Heaven.
Breath of Heaven, lighten my darkness.
Pour over me, Your holiness.
For You are holy, Breath of Heaven.

Jesus Christ gave His life for us. The reason: He loves us so much that He died for us. Even in the wilderness of life and hardships, He is with us. He is holy. He will supply our needs. He will be our comfort. He will meet us where we are and carry us through those difficult times. Sometimes God allows heavy burdens to show us how much we desperately need Him. He will keep His promise to be with us and never leave us.

In Thought

"Dear Lord, I know You are here with me now. You are holy. Help me to release my heavy load and let You carry it for me. You know what's best. Thank You for loving me so much that You gave Your life for me. Amen."

In Word

- *But God showed his great love for us by sending Christ to die for us while we were still sinners.* Romans 5:8 NLT
- *How precious are your thoughts about me, O God. They cannot be numbered! I can't even count them; they outnumber the grains of sand! And when I wake up, you are still with me!* Psalm 139:17-18 NLT

In Deed

If you are weighed down by the problems this world brings, pray and give them to the Lord. Every time a thought about the problem surfaces, pray. Talk to your Father. Pray the words to "Breath of Heaven." Don't take the weight back. The more you pray, the more you will rest in the Lord.

BJ Massa

35
Dig the Hole

We are God's workmanship, created in Christ Jesus to do good works, which God prepared in advance for us to do.
Ephesians 2:10 NIV

When I was younger, every summer brought the same story as the last. The day school let out, my brothers and sister and I would begin pining away for what every child covets at one time or another – a swimming pool. We'd drop hints at first, exaggerating extreme temperature increases and fabricated cases of heat exhaustion. When that didn't work, we'd attempt logic and appeal to our parents' sense of reasoning. And finally, when all of that failed, we'd resort to good old-fashioned whining and complaining.

The strange thing was that no matter our style of appeal, the answer was always the same. The even stranger thing was that the answer was never *no*. In fact, every time the subject came up, my father would say, "Sure! You kids can have a pool any time you want... just dig the hole."

"Dig the what?" We wanted a pool, not an experience in manual labor. To be quite honest, we would have preferred it if he just would have told us no in the first place. A "No" was certainly better than a conditional "Yes." At least with a no, we could have blamed him for our lack of summer fun. Instead, we had to live with the reality that we didn't have a pool, and it was pretty much our own fault.

I don't know what my father would have done if the five of us had actually gotten out there – shovels in hand – and started digging. My guess is that he would have been pretty surprised. But when it came right down to it, he knew us well enough to know that we weren't interested in the process of working for what we wanted; we were just interested in the end result. Dig the hole? Probably not.

How many times have we approached God in the same way a child approaches her father? We pray for Him to bless us. We pray to be used in great and mighty ways. Yet, when He asks us to work for what we want, even just a little, we throw our hands up in the air and give up. When it comes right down to it, we don't want to work for our blessings; we just want to be blessed.

"We are God's workmanship, created in Christ Jesus to do good works, which God prepared in advance for us to do" (Ephesians 2:10 NIV). The Bible is very clear that the Christian life is not a life of lucrative living and bottomless blessings. We are called to be workers – not to attain our salvation but as a result of our salvation.

God wants to bless us. He wants us to have that swimming pool, so to speak. But He also knows that often the greatest blessings are not in the end result, but in the progress of attaining the end result. So when you pray for God to bless you, don't be surprised if He immediately calls you into action. For the real blessing lies not in the swimming pool, but in digging the hole.

In Thought

"Dear Lord, forgive me for all the times You've instructed me to "dig the hole" and I've settled for a mediocre backyard of grass instead. I've been lazy time and time again. I know You created me to do good – even great – works, and I pray that You would open my eyes to the blessings that lie in working for You. It is an honor to be called for Your service, and I pray that my time on this earth would not be wasted. Amen."

In Word

- *Now finish the work, so that your eager willingness to do it may be matched by your completion of it, according to your means.* 2 Corinthians 8:11 NIV
- *Very truly I tell you, whoever believes in me will do the works I have been doing, and they will do even greater things than these, because I am going to the Father.* John 14:12 NIV

In Deed

- Read Matthew 25:14-30 – The Parable of the Talents. What is God's opinion of those who are not willing to work for Him?
- Think of a time when you really had to work for something – school, sports, a job, your marriage. Now forget about the end result – the diploma, the winning game, the promotion, the wedding – and instead think about all of the blessings you received during your preparation for the end result. Do you think the end result would have been as wonderful had you not worked to get there?
- What blessings are you asking God for right now? How is he calling you to action?

Emily Ryan

Week 5 Notes

_____

_____

_____

_____

_____

_____

_____

_____

_____

_____

_____

_____

_____

_____

_____

36
My Will Be Done

Search me, O God, and know my heart;
try me, and know my anxieties.
Psalm 139:23 NKJV

Have you ever really prayed before the Lord? I mean, really fallen before His face and pleaded for Him to answer with a "yes?" We are so often willing to negotiate, beg or act like either answer will be fine with us, when, actually, deep down inside, we just want what we want when we want it!

Like a child, we may even repeat ourselves over and over in the hope that our "perseverance" will reap the reward of getting what we want.

That's how it was one of the many times I prayed that my child would be healed. Oh, as believers, we know that we will all be healed. It's just a matter of when and where. But the location makes all the difference at times. Will our loved ones be healed here or in heaven? We want to *see* that healing.

It was during one of these particular times of prayer that I was pleading with God that He heal my child of his "challenges" so that he would be happy. Clearly a voice said in my head, "How do you know he's not?"

I was stunned. How did I know? Looking at him from the view of the world, I just couldn't see how a child so different from others could be happy. How could he? Oh sure, he laughed a lot, he loved people, he seemed happy...but how could he really have the deep satisfaction of life?

I realized what I really wanted for him was the *joy* that is promised to us through the Holy Spirit (Acts 1:8), rather than happiness, which we are never promised.

The voice of the Lord continued to speak to me, and it went something like, "How do you know that he does not have *more joy* like this than if he met your definition of what would make him happy? How do you know that he's not closer to Me just the way he is?"

Wow! I had been given a parental "talking to" by my heavenly Father, a Father who watched as His only Son "fell short" of what a watching world thought a savior would look like. Yet, our Savior knew the heart of His Father and lived to do His will (John 4:34; 6:38). He didn't have any great accolades or a college degree from Pharisee University. He was simply a man with "nothing in His appearance that we should desire Him" (Isaiah 53:2 NIV). While He was treated with disdain for "bucking the system" in His culture, He was and is the Son of God.

I had been praying for what would be easier for me as a parent rather than for what would bring more glory to His name and very likely more joy to my son. Oh, I still pray for healing, but I know that his pure, sweet relationship with Jesus is everlasting, regardless of his challenges in this life. I know there is a joy that surpasses my understanding in my son's heart for his King.

Are we focusing on our "present trials" on this earth as strangers and aliens here, or are we ever joyful that we are in relationship with the One true and risen Savior?

Take time today to pray over every situation weighing heavy on your heart. Then, pray that the Holy Spirit would take all worry and anxiety from your mind regarding these situations.

In Thought

"Dear Jesus, I know that You know my heart. You knit me in my mother's womb and know the desires of my heart. Please make Your desires my desires. Change my heart and my perspective, and help me to desire You and Your will above all else. Amen."

In Word

* *For your Father knows the things you have need of before you ask Him.* Matthew 6:8 NKJV.
* *Trust in the Lord with all your heart, and lean not on your own understanding; in all your ways acknowledge Him, and He shall direct your paths.* Proverbs 3:5-6 NKJV

In Deed

* Start a prayer journal. It doesn't need to be complicated. Just get a notebook and make a list of your prayer requests each day. Review these requests on a regular basis, and write how and when God answers them.
* Get some newsprint and tack it up in your hallway. Write all the answered prayers from today throughout the end of the year. It will be your record of God's faithfulness. Also note those not answered yet, and even write the answers that are "No" or "Not now."

Kim Lindquist

37

Finding the
Meaning of Mercy

*If you had known what these words mean, "I desire
mercy, not sacrifice," you would not have condemned
the innocent.*
Matthew 12:7 NIV

Mary didn't understand mercy. It was strange to her. Everywhere she
went it seemed that people were always condemning her because she
wasn't what they were—not smart enough, pretty enough, wealthy
enough or in the right circles. Growing up poor on the wrong side of
town, Mary became pregnant at an early age. Everyone she knew
turned their backs on her except Estelle. Mary met Estelle at the
pregnancy center where she'd gone to abort her unwanted child.
Estelle told Mary that God loved her and sent Jesus to die for her, but
Mary didn't understand. Why would God do such a thing for her?
She was nothing. People had been telling her that since she was a
little child, and she just didn't understand how God could love her.

Mary and Estelle became good friends, and Estelle had a compassion
for Mary she'd never experienced before. She explained that Jesus
had changed her life and saved her from drug addiction, and now
she was living for Christ and wanted everyone she met, including
Mary, to come to know Him, too. Initially, Mary wondered if Estelle

was crazy. The day her baby was born, Mary was going to abandon it at the hospital, but Estelle took Mary and the child home with her instead. She helped Mary financially, emotionally and spiritually, and through Estelle's actions and character, Mary saw, and finally began to accept, the mercy of God.

Even though we're called to show mercy to others, many of us still shy away from those who are in need of our help. Sometimes we just don't realize how much a simple act of kindness can impact a person's heart or mind for Christ. How else can the lost see God unless we reflect Him to them in our actions? We are, perhaps, the only Jesus someone may see. Or the only Bible someone may read.

What are others reading in your life today? Do you know what mercy truly is? Isaiah 63:9 says, "In all their affliction He was afflicted, and the angel of His presence saved them; in His love and in His mercy He redeemed them, and He lifted them and carried them all the days of old" (NASB). God showed us mercy by sending Christ to pay a debt we have no way of paying. Christ's mercy for us sent Him to the cross of Calvary. We take up our own cross and follow His example by walking in His merciful, compassionate footsteps and showing His incomparable love to others.

Are you exhibiting the compassion of Christ to those around you? If you find it difficult to show compassion, remember that we can do so in small ways as well as in big ways. A smile to brighten someone's day, a brief word of encouragement to someone under stress, or a helping hand when it is least expected are all simple ways to reach out with the love of Christ.

In Thought

"Dear Lord Jesus, increase my capacity for mercy towards others. Fill me with Your compassion and love, and give me the strength and grace to love others. Instill in me the fruit of Your Holy Spirit so that I may truly reflect You to all who see me. Amen."

In Word

- *Your compassion is great, O LORD.* Psalm 119:156a NIV
- *Blessed are the merciful, for they will be shown mercy.* Matthew 5:7 NIV
- *But because of his great love for us, God, who is rich in mercy, made us alive with Christ even when we were dead in transgressions—it is by grace you have been saved.* Ephesians 2:4-5 NIV

In Deed

- Perform a small act of compassion for someone you know.
- Perform a small act of compassion for someone you don't know.
- Do an attitude check. If your acts of compassion have ulterior motives, ask God to give you compassion for others that is untainted by personal gain.

Patricia Dixon

38

Brownie Bottom Sundae

Lord, if you are willing, you can make me clean.
Luke 5:12b NIV

It was a lazy Sunday afternoon in mid-January, and I was enjoying a post-church gathering of food and football at a friend's house. Not wanting to walk in front of the TV out of respect for the true football fans, I waited for a commercial break to get up and refill my drink. But not two seconds after I stood, three of my girlfriends swarmed around me in a circle so tight I thought maybe the football season had gotten to them and they were forming their own huddle right there in the living room. "Follow me," one whispered and whisked me into the bathroom where she pulled everyone inside and shut the door behind us.

"What's going on?" I asked. "Is this some sort of sports intervention? If so, I'll admit it! I wasn't watching the game!"

They laughed. "I think you sat in something," another managed to get out through the giggles. "Turn around and look in the mirror."

I looked over my shoulder in the mirror and, sure enough, there was half a brownie plastered to the backside of my freshly ironed khakis. I joined in their laugher. "This is gross! I can't believe I didn't see this before I sat down!" I exclaimed, wetting a washcloth to wipe the chocolate off my pants. "I'm so glad y'all didn't let me walk around all day like this, with chocolate squished to my rear!"

"What are friends for?" one friend said, handing me a fresh washcloth. "We know how much you like Brownie Bottom Sundaes, but we figured this was taking it a bit too far!"

It's funny how often we get ourselves into messes without even realizing it. Satan's good like that. It seems like he waits until we're not looking – until we're distracted by the happenings of our lives – and puts something sticky right in our paths. Without fail, we seem to touch it, step in it, or sit in it and walk around foolishly, unaware of our filth. It's so important to look before we sit down, isn't it? To remain alert and aware of our surroundings. Be self-controlled and alert. "Your enemy the devil prowls around like a roaring lion looking for someone to devour," (1 Peter 5:8 NIV).

Likewise, nothing is more valuable than a friend who will tell us when we've sat on a brownie. Or when we have a huge piece of broccoli stuck in our teeth. Or when we're walking around, covered in sin, and we don't even know it – or more sadly, we don't even care. "Better is open rebuke than hidden love. Wounds from a friend can be trusted, but an enemy multiplies kisses," (Proverbs 27:5-6 NIV).

Do you know someone who is in a mess and doesn't know it? Be a true friend and reveal to that person, in love, that they've sat on a brownie. Remind them of the forgiving blood of Christ and help them get clean again. Or perhaps it's you who has stumbled into a messy situation. Don't waste time making excuses for your filth or blaming it on whoever put the mess along your path. Instead, slip away to the foot of the cross, turn on the faucet of God's love, and let Him wash you white as snow.

In Thought

"Dear Lord, forgive me for all those times that I've stumbled into sin so blindly, for the times I've not remained aware and alert like I should. Thank You for my friends who love me enough to tell me when I'm dirty and for Your cleansing blood which You shed on the cross that forgives this sinner time and time again. Amen."

In Word

- *Let us draw near to God with a sincere heart and with the full assurance that faith brings, having our hearts sprinkled to cleanse us from a guilty conscience and having our bodies washed with pure water.* Hebrews 10:22 NIV
- *How much more shall the blood of Christ, who through the eternal Spirit offered Himself without spot to God, cleanse your conscience from dead works to serve the living God?* Hebrews 9:14 NKJV

In Deed

- Examine yourself in the mirror to check for unnoticed sin in your life. Look from all angles. Examine your relationships. Your career. Your thoughts. Your motivations. Your walk with God.
- Ask a close and trusted Christian friend to examine your life from his or her perspective as well, and process any rebuke you receive with a thankful heart.
- If and when you discover that gooey bit of sin on which you've sat, admit it, confess it, let the blood of Christ wash you clean of it, and finally, walk away from it.

Emily Ryan

39
A Hug from Heaven

The Lord is not slow to fulfill his promise as some count slowness, but is patient toward you, not wishing that any should perish, but that all should reach repentance.
2 Peter 3:9 ESV

I set my alarm for 4 a.m. hoping to catch a glimpse of the Leonid Meteor shower that would be visible just before dawn. Because of the nearby city lights, I knew it might not be possible, but I wanted to at least try to see this spectacular light show that God was providing free of charge. The beeping clock roused me and I threw back the covers. It was mid-November, but fall's arrival had been slow and jackets were not yet part of the normal routine. Startled by the chill in the air, I rustled through the hangers in the closet trying to find something to quickly throw across my shoulders before heading outside. My mother's mink coat was the first thing my searching fingers came across so I yanked it off the hanger and slipped my arms into the sleeves.

Outside, I was glad for the extra warmth, and the elegance of mink did not seem inappropriate considering the show I might be seeing. I settled into a patio chair leaning back to search the northeastern sky for streaks of light. I was rewarded with a few, very faint but definite dashes. Although the show wasn't as dramatic as I'd hoped, I was not disappointed. Alone in the clear cool night, I distinctly felt the presence of the One who had created it all: the stars that twinkled overhead, the crisp night air, and the comet named Tempel-Tuttle whose debris had produced the meteors. God's glorious creation was beautifully displayed in the quiet of the early morning.

Then I thought of my mother, now with God, whose coat surrounded me like a hug from heaven. She had given it to me on one of my last visits to her home in Florida. I would never have purchased one for myself, nor do I often have an occasion to wear it. But Mama had lived life extravagantly in every way. Having spent her childhood in near poverty, she seemed to need to affirm to herself and others that she had risen beyond such humble beginnings. What must she think of heaven with streets of gold and a mansion far better than any of her earthly homes? Certainly the luxuries she loved here must appear shabby compared to the extravagant love of God that surrounds her in her real home.

In life Mama had always struggled, not necessarily with hardship, but with herself. She had fought surrendering to God most of her life. Then at 83, she fell and suffered excruciating pain from a broken hip. Because of so many other health issues, surgery was not possible; so she lay in a hospital bed, her leg immobilized. I realized that God had known exactly what she needed. Despite the pain of her last three weeks, they were without a doubt the most peaceful of her life. Finally, surrender had come and with it the peace for which her heart had always longed. I sat by her side reading aloud from the Psalms. In between naps she spoke tenderly to me, regretful of past hurts. It was a sweet time of reconciliation for her - with God and with me. And it was the culmination of over twenty years of prayer for someone whose heart had been hardened by decades of hurt and deception. I was overwhelmed with awe at God's plan and grateful for His patience and unfailing faithfulness.

It's difficult to watch from the sidelines as a loved one struggles with God's best for his or her life. When the months turn into years and the years turn into decades, it's easy to think that God is ignoring our prayers. But He's not. He hears every prayer, and He answers every prayer. No one is beyond reconciliation with God, and time is not an indicator of His ability to soften hearts and change lives. So throw out the calendar and keep praying. God is faithful, and He will act according to His perfect timing.

In Thought

"Lord, Your faithfulness is more than we can comprehend. So often we give up on others when they don't want to hear about You, but You never give up on any of us. No matter what we have done, You love us and want us to choose a life with You. Give us a strong desire to pray for and witness to those who don't yet know You. Amen."

In Word

- *I give thanks to my God always for you because of the grace of God that was given you in Christ Jesus that in every way you were enriched in Him even as the testimony about Christ was confirmed among you so that you are not lacking in any spiritual gift, as you wait for the revealing of our Lord Jesus Christ, who will sustain you to the end, guiltless in the day of our Lord Jesus Christ. 1 Corinthians 1:4-8 ESV*
- *First of all, then, I urge that supplications, prayers, intercessions, and thanksgivings be made for all people, for kings and all who are in high positions, that we may lead a peaceful and quiet life, godly and dignified in every way. This is good, and it is pleasing in the sight of God our Savior, who desires all people to be saved and to come to the knowledge of the truth. 1 Timothy 2:1-4 ESV*

In Deed

Praying for family, friends and acquaintances who have not accepted Christ as Savior is one of the most important tasks we are called to do as believers. Make a list of seven different people who need salvation, and then pray for one each day of the week.

Janie Southard

141

40
Life Begins at The Cross

Is there any encouragement from belonging to Christ? Any comfort from his love? Any fellowship together in the Spirit? Are your hearts tender and compassionate? Then make me truly happy by agreeing wholeheartedly with each other, loving one another, and working together with one mind and purpose. Don't be selfish; don't try to impress others. Be humble, thinking of others as better than yourselves.
Philippians 2:1-3 NLT

My two sons are one and three years old. Their favorite toy in the backyard is a big, blue, plastic car. My mom got a good deal on it at a resale shop. It is a great little car, but all the original placards are torn off and a couple of the corners have obviously been chewed by a dog. The boys love it, though! Its lack of aesthetics does not faze them one bit. This toy is irresistible to them with its open sun roof, steering wheel, storage in the rear and two doors that they love to open and slam shut. Unfortunately, the car seats only one passenger, so there is always a constant battle of who will be the driver. I am always amazed how this brings out the worst in both of them. They start out playing peacefully, but in the end, one of them ends up getting pushed out of one of the doors and then proceeds to cry a puddle of tears. That is when playtime is over and the toy gets put in the garage!

could see where a group was building a casket for the baby who had died. All the other people were sitting around reading the tracts that had been given to them. The Chief came back to Milton and Jim and asked them to tell the people about the tract.

No air had been moving up to this point. Then a gentle wind started to blow. Milton and Jim took turns talking. They explained the tract the people had been reading. They offered the plan of salvation. They invited those who would like to pray to receive Jesus as their Lord and Savior into their heart to follow them in a prayer. After the prayer they asked how many had prayed and half of the people raised their hands, approximately 150 people, with the Chief being among them.

Then as quickly as they were allowed to come, Milton and Jim were asked to leave the area. The perfect window of opportunity had come and now it was over. God had a plan for that day and He used Milton and Jim to fulfill His purpose.

How many times in our lives are we given opportunities to do a mighty work for our Lord and let the opportunity slip through our fingers? Or how many opportunities do we allow to sit on the shelf, so to speak, thinking that some day we plan to get around to doing something about them when we have more time? One very important factor in this story is that when Milton and Jim were first told they could not go to the gathering, they did not give up and go away. They prayed and waited for God for the next step to take. It is of utmost importance to pray and then listen for instruction.

In Thought

"Lord, thank You for Your guidance in all that we do. Please give us clear instructions regarding what You want us to do to glorify You including how to do it. Let us be Your instrument. We love You and want to serve You and be in Your will. Amen."

In Word

- *Consequently, faith comes from hearing the message, and the message is heard through the word of Christ.* Romans 10:17 NIV
- *I am not ashamed of the gospel, because it is the power of God for the salvation of everyone who believes.* Romans 1:16 NIV
- *For God, who said, "Let light shine out of darkness," made his light shine in our hearts to give us the light of the knowledge of the glory of God in the face of Christ.* 2 Corinthians 4:6 NIV

In Deed

- Be aware of needs when you see them and seize the opportunity to take care of them.
- Try not to procrastinate about doing things. If we all wait for a rainy day to get anything done, we may be in for a pretty big flood.
- Understand that volunteering is not just for other people. Anybody can do it.

Sharon Rigsby

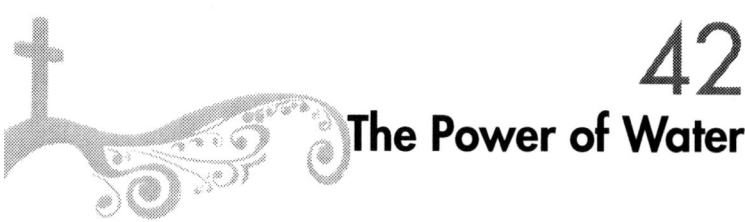

42
The Power of Water

Jesus answered her, "If you knew the gift of God and who it is that asks you for a drink, you would have asked him and he would have given you living water."
John 4:10 NIV

Until June of 2001, I had never met Bonnie and Lyle. But when Tropical Storm Allison buried their home in over six feet of water, it didn't matter that we were strangers. It just mattered that their home was destroyed, and they needed all the help they could find to salvage some of their personal belongings.

The majority of their possessions were ruined, piled in the front yard to be hauled away by garbage men. And inside the house, the stench was so potent that it didn't just stop at my nose; it stung my eyes and burned my lungs and made me want to give up that suddenly annoying, life-sustaining habit of breathing.

But in the midst of the devastation, I found myself in their back yard, hunched over a plastic kiddie pool filled with water and Palmolive, scrubbing mud off their plates, cups, pots and pans. Those, at least, could be saved.

The sun was beating down on my neck and the bubbles were climbing up my arms as I scrubbed when the irony of the moment hit me. Just a few days earlier, there was one thing Bonnie and Lyle feared – water. Its potential to destroy threatened their material belongings, their shelter, and even their very lives. It had power unlike anything they had ever seen and demanded that all in its wake stop and take notice of its might.

But then, just a few days later, water took on a completely different role in their lives. The water they once feared became the very thing they needed to start their lives over again in the aftermath of the storm. It had the power to renew, refresh, and completely cleanse like nothing else could. The water, which had the power to destroy, also had the power to save. It seemed a paradox.

So, too, do God's justice and God's mercy seem to be a paradox.

God's power is immeasurable. He alone holds infinite potential, infinite strength and infinite might, and it is for those reasons we should fear Him. This isn't the type of fear that should lead to a God-phobia of sorts, but the kind of fear that reflects our respect for His awesomeness.

But along with His infinite power comes His infinite grace, for He alone has the ability to cleanse us. We are dirty, filthy and caked with sin, just like Bonnie and Lyle's dishes were caked with mud. We need Him to cleanse us as only He can.

When Christ offered the woman at the well "living water" (John 4), He was offering her a way to be forgiven and washed as white as snow. He offers us the same thing. We can choose to accept the living water and the saving power it brings, or we can choose to reject it and face the Lord's destructive power instead.

In Thought

"Dear God, thank You for Your cleansing power that You displayed on the cross. I pray that I would be forever mindful of the awe and respect that You deserve and never take Your grace for granted. Amen."

In Word

- *Wash away all my iniquity and cleanse me from my sin.* Psalm 51:2 NIV
- *Your impurity is your lewdness and the corruption of your idolatry. I tried to cleanse you, but you refused. So now you will remain in your filth until my fury against you has been satisfied.* Ezekiel 24:13 NLT
- *In fact, the law requires that nearly everything be cleansed with blood, and without the shedding of blood there is no forgiveness.* Hebrews 9:22 NIV

In Deed

- When watching the weather reports, pay close attention to all of the warnings given for various threats of water like hurricanes, tsunamis, blizzards, etc.
- At the same time, pay close attention to how much you depend on water and need water on a daily basis.
- The next time you struggle with understanding God's justice and His mercy, remember how those two characteristics of water coexist so seamlessly.

Emily Ryan

149

Week 6 Notes

_____

_____

_____

_____

_____

_____

_____

_____

_____

_____

_____

_____

_____

_____

_____

43
The Rain Dance

Every good and perfect gift is from above, coming down from the Father of the heavenly lights, who does not change like shifting shadows.
James 1:17 NIV

The family across the street from us when I was growing up was my second family. I was and still am blessed to be an honorary member of their family! The youngest son, Steve, and I often played together. At times, our friendship was very much like that of true siblings. We'd pick on each other, argue and come up with some crazy ideas.

One summer day when the heat was high (a typical Houston summer), we decided it needed to rain. We picked the big oak tree in our front yard as the site for our "rain dance." We just knew it would work. I don't know how long we danced around that tree in true American Indian fashion, complete with whooping and hollering! I do remember, though, that we were pretty persistent!

Imagine our delight when it began to rain! Of course, we told anyone who would listen what we had done! We took full credit for this act of nature. Had it not been for us, it could have been weeks and weeks before we saw any precipitation.

My mother, as always, was indulging. Never once did she bring up any weather forecasts she may have heard on the news. Nor was there any mention of any clouds that may have been in the sky before our monumental task.

We simply took full credit.

How often do we still take credit as the workers of miracles today? We may quickly tell friends how much we prayed for them when we hear that our prayer was answered. We may thank the doctor for healing our loved one. Or we may pat ourselves on the back for getting out of debt. Occasionally, we thank and praise the Lord as an afterthought.

The Lord, alone, is the Answerer of prayer, the Healer of disease, the Deliverer from sin. I wonder what goes through His mind when we declare our victories in prayer without making Him the focus of the miracle!

Not once in Scripture do we read "in the name of Paul" or "Luke the Christ." Miracles done and words spoken by the apostles and disciples of Jesus Christ pointed back to Jesus as the source of all power! As His disciples, we are to do the same in our actions and in our speech.

In Thought

"Dear Jesus, thank You for Your patience with me. Put a check in my spirit when I take too much pride in myself rather than taking pride in You, Your work, and Your ways! May I give You the glory in everything! Amen."

In Word

- *Oh, give thanks to the LORD! Call upon His name; make known His deeds among the peoples!* 1 Chronicles 16:8 NKJV
- *But thanks be to God, who gives us the victory through our Lord Jesus Christ.* 1 Corinthians 15:57 NKJV

In Deed

Make a list of all the "good and perfect gifts" given to you by the Lord. Now, make a list of all of the difficult things, situations and people in your life that God is allowing to be there. Take time to praise Him in all these things, remembering that He is in control.

Kim Lindquist

44

It's the Real Thing

All Scripture is God-breathed and is useful for teaching, rebuking, correcting and training in righteousness, so that the servant of God may be thoroughly equipped for every good work.
2 Timothy 3:16-17 NIV

When I was a teenager, my family took a trip to our nation's capital, Washington D.C. I had completed American history that year in school, so I was excited to see and touch what I had only read about in books. It really was an amazing experience. I will never forget touring the Capitol building, White House, Lincoln Memorial, Jefferson Memorial, as well as the Smithsonian Museums, just to name a few! My enthusiasm dampened, however, when I was told one morning at breakfast that we were going to the Treasury Department's Bureau of Engraving and Printing. I remember asking my parents, "Why there, who comes to Washington D.C. and goes to the Bureau of Engraving and Printing? Why are we going to waste half a day looking at printed money that we can't even touch?" My complaints were heard and quickly dismissed.

The tour was not as bad as I had feared. We watched as the United States paper currency was printed, stacked, cut and examined for defects. I was amazed at these federal employees who sat eight hours a day at a table and examined many pages of newly printed money. After what seemed like seconds, the examiner would move from sheet to sheet, and every so often, would throw away what seemed to my eyes to be perfectly good money. This amazed me! How could these examiners know so quickly that that money was not perfect? It looked great to me!

Sensing our questions, our tour guide explained it to us. He said the examiner is able to look at the large sheets of newly printed money and see the defects instantly because of the way they were trained. They spent their first full year examining nothing but the real thing. They became so familiar with what a bill should look like that they could instantly recognize any money that was not perfect. They readily know if it's the real thing!

As Christians beginning our walk with the Lord, we should spend our first years engrossed in the Bible, knowing it from cover to cover. It is the inerrant Word of God that is the standard for all followers of Christ. When we know the truth, it is easy to recognize things that are false and inaccurate. Those things stand out boldly like a red flag and readily show themselves to go against what God has said in the Bible.

In Thought
"Lord, thank You for giving me unlimited access to truth in the form of Jesus Christ and the Bible. Help me to read and understand the Scriptures and apply them to my life daily. I pray that You give me wisdom and discernment that can only come from You. Amen."

In Word
Deal with your servant according to your love and teach me your decrees. I am your servant; give me discernment that I may understand your statutes. Psalm 119:124-125 NIV

In Deed
Start today to dive into the Scriptures and teachings of the Bible. Remember, it is the anointed, inspired and infallible Word of God. Pray daily that God gives you discernment to recognize the truth as the real thing.

Mikelle Challenger

45
Got God?

If you do what is right, will you not be accepted? But if you do not do what is right, sin is crouching at your door; it desires to have you, but you must master it.
Genesis 4:7 NIV

Think back to high school; for some of you it might be more recent than others of us. Were you accepted back then? Were you someone who played by the rules or were you the rebel who was just trying to fit in with a specific crowd? I really didn't associate with a certain crowd. I wasn't popular, and I surely didn't think I was very pretty. What I didn't realize back then was that I was already accepted by God. He wasn't concerned with my popularity status; He just wanted me to have a personal relationship with Him. I was saved at an early age, but I was far from living a life that honored Christ. So as anyone trying to fit in, I found ways that I thought were attracting the right people. As my senior year rolled around and after graduation, sin was totally at my door – it didn't even have to knock anymore.

I began drinking before the legal age of 21 and when I did, I felt in control and more accepted by the world around me. I was getting the attention of boys and that made me feel pretty. As a child of God, I'm supposed to lean only on Him to satisfy my every desire, and it's only He who can make me feel complete. It's our eternal life with Christ that is important; not the things of this earth that are full of sin and heartache. Our sin, if we let it, will master us and mine has for many years.

I'm not going to beat around the bush; get up, get God and get your life on the right path for acceptance in the kingdom of your heavenly Father who loves and adores you just as you are!

In Thought

"Oh Father, thank You so much for the mercy and grace You have given me over the years and through the many times my back was turned to You. You never left me. You kept tugging at my heart and continually showed me Your love and acceptance for me as your child. I pray for those who are searching for acceptance from everyone and everything but You. Help them discover the same healing You've given me, and help them know that You love them no matter what their past looks like. Amen."

In Word

- *Accept one another, then, just as Christ accepted you, in order to bring praise to God.* Romans 15:7 NIV
- *Those who live according to the sinful nature have their minds set on what that nature desires; but those who live in accordance with the Spirit have their minds set on what the Spirit desires.* Romans 8:5 NIV
- *Do not conform any longer to the pattern of this world, but be transformed by the renewing of your mind. Then you will be able to test and approve what God's will is – his good, pleasing and perfect will.* Romans 12:2 NIV

In Deed

Instead of trying to fit in at the work place or at school by wearing the right name brands or driving the right car; choose to follow Christ's instructions laid out for us in His Word and strive to be holy as He is holy.

Cindy Cañas

46
Grape Jelly and Fruitfulness

So, my dear brothers and sisters, be strong and immovable. Always work enthusiastically for the Lord, for you know that nothing you do for the Lord is ever useless.
1 Corinthians 15:58 NLT

My husband and I have always had grape vines in our backyard. After a particularly good crop of grapes several years ago, his parents and grandmother (GiGi) came over to teach us how to make grape jelly. GiGi brought a few of her ancient cooking tools that were necessary for an old-fashioned craft such as canning, and I was fascinated with these kitchen items that I had never seen before. She had a cone-shaped colander and a cone-shaped wooden piece to mash the grapes in the colander. In a day of microwaves and George Foreman grilles, they aren't exactly the kind of items a couple registers for when they get engaged.

Imagine our joy when we were at an estate sale a few months later and found our very own grape-squashing tools just like GiGi's! We snatched them up in a heartbeat and were so happy we found such a treasure before anyone else did. When jelly-making time came around again, we borrowed GiGi's tools and paired them with our own so we could both mash grapes together.

Immediately, we noticed a huge difference in the two sets of tools. The set we got from the estate sale was shiny and new, with a sparkling silver colander and a wooden piece that was perfectly smooth and a beautiful shade of light golden brown. In comparison, his grandma's tools were dull and worn, with a wooden cone that was stained a deep royal shade of purple. Clearly, one set had been used repeatedly while the other had been buried in the dark corner of a kitchen cabinet.

As I looked at the two sets side by side, at first the newer set seemed to be more appealing to me. It seemed nice and clean and very "Williams-Sonoma-ish." But, then I realized that his grandma's tools displayed years and years of being used for a specific purpose. They had been productive and fruitful and demonstrated a lifetime of usefulness. It wasn't that they were dirty or ruined or even worn out. Instead, they had been used for the exact purpose for which they had been made, and that alone made them beautiful.

It's easy to look in the mirror sometimes and see ourselves as worn out or "ruined." Maybe our bodies aren't what they used to be after years of having children. Maybe our homes are not as organized as we'd like because of the hours spent working or serving elsewhere. Maybe our hands are calloused or our skin is wrinkled from years of working outside in the sun.

But the truth is that work is a part of God's plan and His purpose for all of us, and when we don't work to the best of our abilities, we're sinning against Him. "Never be lazy, but work hard and serve the Lord enthusiastically" (Romans 12:11 NLT). The Bible never tolerates the "cruise control" kind of lifestyle. Instead, it commands a life of hard work, diligent service and enthusiastic initiative.

Don't strive to get to the end of your life and still see yourself with a shiny, new finish. Instead, strive to look back and see a life that is a little dull, a little worn, with accents that are stained a deep, royal purple. Strive for a life that has been used by God. A life that displays His fruitfulness.

In Thought

"Dear Lord, Help me to see You as my boss in everything I do. Help me work for You diligently, and forgive my times of laziness. I pray that my work would be honoring to You, and that You would bless the fruits of my labor. Amen."

In Word

- *Whatever your hand finds to do, do it with all your might, for in the grave, where you are going, there is neither working nor planning nor knowledge nor wisdom.* Ecclesiastes 9:10 NIV
- *I have brought you glory on earth by completing the work you gave me to do.* John 17:4 NIV
- *And we pray this in order that you may live a life worthy of the Lord and may please him in every way: bearing fruit in every good work, growing in the knowledge of God.* Colossians 1:10 NIV
- *Whatever you do, work at it with all your heart, as working for the Lord, not for men...* Colossians 3:23 NIV
- *Work hard so you can present yourself to God and receive his approval. Be a good worker, one who does not need to be ashamed and who correctly explains the word of truth.* 2 Timothy 2:15 NLT
- *Work with enthusiasm, as though you were working for the Lord rather than for people.* Ephesians 6:7 NLT

In Deed

- Look at your schedule and see if you are using your time wisely. Are there certain activities you could cut out in order to be more productive?
- While rest is just as important as hard work, the ratio of work to rest that God demonstrates is in Genesis 6:1 – six days of work compared to one day of rest. When you analyze your work-to-rest ratio, does it come close to God's example for us? If not, what can you do to change that?

Emily Ryan

47
The Still, Small Voice

Be still, and know that I am God.
Psalm 46:10a ESV

I'd always heard that by the time you're 40, you should be doing what you love to do. So after being out of work for over two years, I started my own business as a freelance writer. Freelance means I'm my own boss. I set my own hours. Work when I want to. Work when I *have* to. I registered my business and my website and got busy looking for writing jobs. I got my office all set up, the proper software loaded on my computer, hanging files in the desk, and all the necessary tax forms and the DBA form from the county. I spent a lot of time getting it going, including hours each day getting my name out there and doing everything in my power to make this a successful venture. There was only one thing I wasn't doing: writing.

I need total quiet to read or write. If there's any background noise at all, I can't concentrate. I can't write in a dirty house, either. If I can find something to do around the house, I'll go do it instead of planting myself in the chair and doing my job.

After some time, I had a few writing gigs but wasn't really getting anywhere. I spent time in prayer asking the Lord for guidance and for work to come my way. I was also experiencing some serious writer's block at the time so I prayed for ideas as well.

One night, I woke up at 3 a.m. suddenly full of article ideas, devotional ideas, essay ideas, and ways to market my business. Knowing myself, I knew I had to get up and write it all down quickly before I dozed back off and erased my memory.

It hit me that I should have started with prayer and seeking God first. Why do we always make prayer the last resort? It should be our starting point. Our launching pad. Don't pass go, don't collect $200, don't do anything until you've handed it to God and aligned your will to His. After all, that's what prayer really is for. It's not coming up with the magic formula to get God to do what we want. It's for us to get in on what He's doing and ditching our agenda in favor of His. Personal initiative is no substitute for reliance upon God.

That whole "pray without ceasing" thing? It doesn't mean walking around with our eyes closed murmuring to ourselves. The world thinks we're strange enough already! It has much more to do with listening and waiting. It means having our heads on a swivel and our hearts and ears open. I envision it as having an antenna on top of your head, or a satellite dish, ready to pick up His signal at any moment.

My kids love to go hang out at the large, 170-foot cross that sits on the grounds of our church. My youngest is really into rockets, so he sometimes jokes that he wishes the area around the cross was a launching pad and at the end of the countdown, the cross would just blast off! Metaphorically speaking, he's onto something. The cross should be where we launch our ideas and bring our requests. Our home plate, so to speak.

A sign hanging on a wall in our house says: "A day stitched in prayer seldom unravels." I like that. I think I'll move it and put it above my writing desk. You know....just in case writer's block sets in again.

In Thought

"Father, forgive me for doing things on my own because I am *not* my own. I'm bought with a precious price. I am Yours. You are my Lord and I am to follow You. Help me to be a better listener. Amen."

In Word

- *Come now, you who say, "Today or tomorrow we will go into such and such a town and spend a year there and trade and make a profit" — yet you do not know what tomorrow will bring. What is your life? For you are a mist that appears for a little time and then vanishes. Instead you ought to say, "If the Lord wills, we will live and do this or that." As it is, you boast in your arrogance. All such boasting is evil. So whoever knows the right thing to do and fails to do it, for him it is sin.* James 4:13-17 ESV

- *Do not be anxious about anything, but in everything by prayer and supplication with thanksgiving let your requests be made known to God. And the peace of God, which surpasses all understanding, will guard your hearts and your minds in Christ Jesus.* Philippians 4:6-7 ESV

In Deed

Most of us have a to-do list or a daily calendar, like a Franklin Planner. Look over your to-do list and make it your prayer list. Pray over those items each morning and let the Holy Spirit guide you as you perform your daily tasks. He may tell you to work harder or faster or slower or more carefully, or He may change your agenda completely.

Dwight Baker

48
Somebody May Be Watching You

They went out and preached that people should repent.
Mark 6:12 NIV

Dominica is an island nation in the Caribbean Sea. When you say that name, many people assume you are speaking of the Dominican Republic, but they are definitely two different locations. Dominica is located north-northwest of Guadeloupe and to the southeast of Martinique. It is the youngest island in the Lesser Antilles. Its capital is Roseau, and it has 750 square miles with a population of about 72,500. Dominica features lush, mountainous, rain forests, and many rare plant, animal and bird species. Its economy is heavily dependent on both agriculture and tourism.

But that is not why we were there.

A few years ago, I was part of a team that went to Dominica to do two things. One was to present medical supplies to a hospital to replace those that had been lost in a fire. The other was to do door-to-door and street evangelism.

I had only been involved with missions for a couple of years at that time, so one-on-one witnessing was still pretty new to me. Each day we would begin with a devotion and prayer and by the time we set out for the streets, I can honestly say that I felt no fear. As God's strength filled me, I felt a peace that I would be given the words that He would have me say in His perfect timing.

One experience will always stand out in my memories. We had been visiting and talking with people in the town square for a while. Our group had experienced many good conversations with people all morning. For some reason, I felt an urging to go to the corner of the square and take the path leading down to the boat dock about a block away. As I walked, I could see a fisherman in a boat just coming back to the dock. I walked up to him as he was tying up his boat and began to talk with him. I shared Jesus with him and explained that he could have Jesus in his heart. I don't remember the exact words I said to him because, at a time like that, the Holy Spirit takes over and speaks for you. I do remember distinctly asking him if he would like to pray to receive Jesus into his heart and he said, "Yes." He prayed and asked Jesus to forgive him and save him. I gave him some material to read and he thanked me. As I turned to leave, a young man who had been behind us approached me and said, "I would like to say the prayer." He had been listening all along. He needed the message also.

I realized then that wherever you are, the things you are doing or saying are affecting not only the person in front of you, but some people you may never even know about this side of heaven. I was blessed to see and hear about this one. Next time, maybe not. But the seed may be planted. I just pray that I will always be casting out the seeds wherever I go.

In Thought

"Lord, thank You for giving us eternal life through Your Son, Jesus Christ. Empower us to take that precious message of life to others at every opportunity. Help us be willing to be used by You. Amen."

In Word

- *He personally carried the load of our sins in his own body when he died on the cross, so that we can be finished with sin and live a good life from now on. For his wounds have healed ours!* 1 Peter 2:24 TLB
- *For whoever does the will of my Father in heaven is my brother and sister and mother.* Matthew 12:50 NIV
- *The Lord is close to the brokenhearted and saves those who are crushed in spirit.* Psalm 34:18 NIV

In Deed

Be conscious of your actions and your words today, paying close attention to those who may be listening or watching you from afar.

Sharon Rigsby

167

49
Show Me a Sign

Then Jesus told him, "Because you have seen me, you have believed; blessed are those who have not seen and yet have believed."
John 20:29 NIV

A high fever coupled with a glassy-eyed stare from a child who is too young to communicate is a combination of symptoms no parent ever wants to encounter. So when my 22-month-old son, Canaan, transformed from a bouncing, bubbly toddler into a lethargic, unresponsive little boy in a matter of an hour, my husband and I made a frantic trip to the emergency room for some answers. After several tests, blood work, x-rays, and an IV drip, Canaan remained unchanged; and we were no closer to figuring out the source of his condition than we were when we arrived.

Several hours later, I found myself strapped to a hospital gurney with Canaan in my arms being wheeled into the back of an ambulance at three o'clock in the morning because he was being transferred to Texas Children's Hospital where they hoped the pediatric unit would be able to provide more answers.

As I felt the heat radiating from his little body, I tried desperately to keep every possible worst case scenario from playing out in my mind. I prayed that God would heal him. I prayed for answers. And I prayed for some sign that all of my desperate pleas were being heard.

I knew we would be traveling north on the freeway; and depending on my position in the ambulance and the angle of the windows, there was a small chance I'd be able to see our church's 170-foot tall cross spotlighted in the darkness. Oh how I wanted to see that cross! I watched familiar landmarks fly by the windows and craned my neck for just a glimpse of the cross when I could tell we were close. But I never saw it.

At first, I was devastated. All I wanted was a simple "sign" that God was listening, but instead I got nothing. I felt lost, alone, forgotten and scared. If I couldn't "see" God, then surely He couldn't see me.

But almost as soon as the thought formulated in my mind, the truth of God's Word swept in and set me straight. I didn't need to see a cross to know that God was listening. I also didn't need to "feel" His presence to know that He had never left my side. I understood then that faith is knowing that the reality of who God is is not dependent upon my perception of Him.

I never did get a "sign" that my little boy would be all right. Instead we left the hospital 24 hours later with a perfectly healthy child and no answers as to why he had been so sick. I learned then that the absence of a sign from God does not equate to the absence of God.

Have you ever prayed for a sign before? Almost all of us have. The truth is, sometimes we get those signs that we pray for, like Gideon did in Judges 6, or like the sign of the rainbow in Genesis 9. But other times God asks us just to trust Him and believe, even when our eyes cannot see Him, our ears do not hear Him, and our fingers cannot reach out and feel the evidence of His goodness.

Because we all go through times that God feels invisible or apathetic to us, we must prepare for those times in advance by strengthening our faith through His Word. How well do you really know what the Bible says about your God? Immerse yourself now in the truth of His Word so that the next time God seems invisible to you, the truth will eclipse any doubts you may have. You may still find yourself praying for a "sign," but don't be surprised when that sign is simply His Word manifesting itself clearly and lovingly into your heart.

In Thought

"Dear God, please forgive me for the times when I've treated You like a genie and demanded that You show Yourself to me at the exact times I request. Help me remember that I answer to You; You do not answer to me. And I pray that You will bless my time in Your Word so that I may grow to know You, and therefore, trust You more and more every day. Amen."

In Word

- *For in this hope we were saved. But hope that is seen is no hope at all. Who hopes for what he already has? But if we hope for what we do not yet have, we wait for it patiently.* Romans 8:24-25 NIV
- *Now faith is confidence in what we hope for and assurance about what we do not see.* Hebrews 11:1 NIV
- *Though you have not seen him, you love him; and even though you do not see him now, you believe in him and are filled with an inexpressible and glorious joy, for you are receiving the goal of your faith, the salvation of your souls.* 1 Peter 1:8-9 NIV

In Deed

- Pinpoint the exact place in your life where God seems to be silent, and then search the Scriptures for verses on that topic. Use your concordance for help.
- Go to a Christian bookstore and find some material on the different names of God used in the Bible. Getting to know Him as He refers to Himself in His Word is a great way to strengthen your faith.

Emily Ryan

Week 7 Notes

_____

_____

_____

_____

_____

_____

_____

_____

_____

_____

_____

_____

_____

_____

_____

50
I Know Him!

*And let us consider how to stir up one another to love
and good works, not neglecting to meet together, as is
the habit of some, but encouraging one another, and all
the more as you see the Day drawing near.*
Hebrews 10:24-25 ESV

One of my favorite Christmas movies is *Elf* starring Will Ferrell. It's
one of those movies I can watch over and over again. Watching it
with someone who hasn't seen it is almost unfair because I'm trying to
stifle a laugh before the joke even comes. A running gag we have at
the house is every time one of us or someone on TV mentions Santa
we scream, "Santa! I know him! I know him!"

We've all heard sermons where we were asked if we really knew
Jesus or just knew *about* Him. Lots of people know *about* Jesus;
they've heard the stories or remember what they were taught in
Sunday school as children. They know facts, historical events, the
names of His disciples, etc. Some even believe beyond a shadow of a
doubt that He actually existed. When asked if they "believe in Jesus,"
they think you're asking about His mere existence, akin to asking if
they believe in the Easter Bunny or the Tooth Fairy.

A man once told me that he'd learned more about God since leaving
the church than he ever did while attending church. His point was,

why attend church? You don't *have* to go to church to be a Christian. In his mind, it had actually done him harm. The setting wasn't one where I could openly talk to him further about it, but I think I know what I'd ask him if I ever got the chance again:

- *Which* God do you refer to, the God of the Bible? The same God that commands we stay involved with His Church in a body of believers to encourage one another and make sure we're staying true to His Word? (*Hebrews 10:23-25 ESV*)
- *How* have you learned about God, through trial and error, personal experiences, observing others (who may or may not be true followers)?
- *When* you do read the Bible, do you understand what you're reading? Do you comprehend the overall message? How do you know you're interpreting it correctly? Can you tell the difference between historical narrative, poetry, prophecy or wisdom literature?
- I'd ask him how he knows *I'm* not leading him astray. In other words, what's he anchored to, the Word or his subjective experience and opinion?

I'd ask him these questions to make the point that there are no "Lone Ranger" Christians. Nobody gets to go it alone and make up whatever version of Christianity suits him or her. Christianity is a team sport; it must be lived in concert with other followers to ensure we haven't strayed from the true faith.

In Thought

"Dear Lord, I want to know You fully as You know me fully. I don't simply want to know about You; I want a personal relationship with You so that You can live through me. I want You to be the first one I run to when trouble comes, not a last resort. Amen."

In Word

In reading this, then, you will be able to understand my insight into the mystery of Christ. Ephesians 3:4 NIV

In Deed

- Analyze your church attendance. If it is sporadic at best, make a list of the things that keep you from attending on a regular basis. Now ask God to help you prioritize those obligations and/or distractions.
- If you are not a member of a Bible study class, start visiting one this coming Sunday and resolve to make that a part of your Sunday morning routine as well.

Dwight Baker

51
It's All About Presentation

Blessed are those who hunger and thirst for righteousness for they shall be satisfied.
Matthew 5:6 NASB

I was about seven when I first noticed that making an appetizing presentation was an important aspect when it comes to food. After school I had walked next door to see if my friend could come out to play. There she sat in her living room before a black and white cartoon of Yogi Bear. What struck my eyes, though, was the color on the TV tray before her. Artfully arranged on a plate were several lightly browned crackers each covered with a small piece of perfectly square orange cheese; a frosty green bottle of 7-Up sat alongside. Perhaps I was just hungry, but I looked longingly at what appeared to be a display of culinary pizzazz.

To my eyes it held the same fascination as a juicy steak would to a starving cowboy. At that moment, I decided that in the future I would like all my snacks to have the same appealing look. Home from school the next day, I asked my mother if she could prepare just such a tray for me. I'm sure she must have thought I'd suffered some sort of head trauma on the playground. She stared down at me for a moment searching intently for any facial bruising and simply said, "No."

A few years later, I carefully emptied the china cabinet of her deep green plates with the large gardenia in the middle. Some of my friends had spent the night, and I was certain they would be impressed if I served our breakfast of pop tarts and cantaloupe on them. My mother patiently tolerated my flamboyance and waited until everyone had left before she reminded me that we would now have to hand wash all the delicate dishes.

As an adult, I've continued my pursuit to make food as attractive as it is delicious. I delight in creating dazzling desserts for my family and friends. I've learned how to make a chocolate ganache and drizzle it haphazardly down the sides of a layer cake and then garnish it with plump red strawberries. From estate sales and thrift shops I have collected an array of serving dishes from silver to crystal upon which to display my edible art. While I carefully choose my recipes and use quality ingredients, it is the way in which the final product is delivered that enhances their appeal and causes the salivary glands of onlookers to begin their churning.

It's just the same with righteousness. Matthew 5:6 tells us, "Blessed are those who hunger and thirst for righteousness for they shall be satisfied" (NASB). If we want unbelievers to hunger and thirst for God, our presentation is of utmost importance. But the appealing look we seek to present can come only from the inside. It is what Peter describes as "the hidden person of the heart, with the imperishable quality of a gentle and quiet spirit" (1 Peter 3:4 NASB). And there's only one recipe book with instructions for this appetizing dish - the Bible.

In Thought

"Lord, create in me a desire to cultivate a gentle and quiet spirit that will be an accurate and tasteful presentation of You to others. Then help me to get out of the way and allow You to use me to reveal Yourself to them. Amen."

In Word

- *How will they preach unless they are sent? Just as it is written, "How beautiful are the feet of those who bring good news of good things!"* Romans 10:15 NASB
- *Be diligent to present yourself approved to God as a workman who does not need to be ashamed, accurately handling the word of truth.* 2 Timothy 2:15 NASB
- *Your adornment must not be merely external – braiding the hair, and wearing gold jewelry, or putting on dresses; but let it be the hidden person of the heart, with the imperishable quality of a gentle and quiet spirit, which is precious in the sight of God.* 1 Peter 3:3-4 NASB

In Deed

- Think about how you are presenting Christ to others. Consider your wardrobe – are you dressing appropriately? Consider your work ethic – are you quick to go above and beyond for a project? Consider your Facebook updates – are you frequently complaining?
- Ask God to reveal to you any areas of your life in which you are not being an accurate reflection of His righteousness.

Janie Southard

52
God's Instrument

---

*In his heart a man plans his course, but the Lord
determines his steps.*
Proverbs 16:9 NIV

A few years ago my husband, Frank, and I were privileged to lead teams to the Bush of Zambia to evangelize the people there. To prepare our teams, we had extensive training sessions before each trip. We covered everything from preaching preparation, adult lessons, children lessons, crafts, culture, history, immunizations, testimonies, witnessing, prayer-walking, health issues, clothing and itinerary to scheduling and much more. We even prepared to have eyeglass clinics in the villages. By the time our teams left, we were trained and ready to do God's work.

Like Psalm 16:9 says, a man makes plans and that is a good thing; but then the Lord takes over and directs his steps. You prepare and then the Lord can use you. There were countless times on the trip that we had meticulous plans laid out for the day and the Lord took over and did it completely His way. He still used all the skills we had learned in our training. He just did it His way instead.

One day, part of our team went to a remote village named Gocho. They met under big mango trees because every time they tried to build a structure for worship, it washed away in the yearly floods during the rainy season. Several of us worked with the children playing games, singing, performing dramas, and teaching Bible stories and verses.

Frank and others worked with the adults.

Frank had worked on several different sermons that he had planned to use. Using a translator, he began his planned speech, but right away he began to feel that he needed to go off script. God's message began to come from him naturally as if he had planned the alternative speech all along.

That day the eyeglass clinic was at Gocho also. As subsistence farmers with a yearly income equivalent to only one hundred dollars, these people are extremely poor. They live in huts with dirt floors and thatch roofs. In order to have their eyes examined they had to pay a very small fee (5000 Kwacha, the equivalent of $1.50).

Frank told the people that they should help each other whenever they saw someone in need if it was a need that they could meet. While teaching, Frank saw an elderly gentleman at the back of the crowd who was having trouble reading his Bible. He said to the man, "If my brother here does not have the money to have his eyes examined, but I do, then I should offer it to him." And Frank took the money out of his pocket and gave it to the man. The man thanked him and went to the eyeglass clinic area nearby while Frank continued teaching. Eighteen people accepted the Lord as their Savior that day, and by the time Frank finished teaching, the man returned with his new glasses, which turned out to be a very specific trifocal prescription we just happened to have.

A few minutes later the man approached Frank. Over his shoulder he had a beautifully woven six-foot circular mat made of strips of corn husks. The man made these for his hut floor. It was all he had to give, so he gave this mat to Frank. It reminded me of the widow's mite (Mark 12:41-44). God can take a willing open heart and use it.

God wants you to be prepared for His work. He wants you to study His Word. Then He can take you and use you. He just needs you to go and open your mouth and let His words come out. Then His blessings will flow back all over you. That mat is still a reminder to Frank and me of God's blessings if we allow Him to use us as His instruments.

In Thought

"Lord, thank You for Your Word and how You teach us what You want us to teach others. Help us to look for ways to serve You and share Your message and be Your instrument. Lord, use us any way at any time and may all the glory go to You. Amen."

In Word

- *Study to show thyself approved unto God, a workman that needeth not to be ashamed, rightly dividing the word of truth.* 2 Timothy 2:15 KJV
- *The Lord will fulfill his purpose for me; your love, O Lord, endures forever—do not abandon the works of your hands.* Psalm 138:8 NIV
- *So that Christ may dwell in your hearts through faith. And I pray that you, being rooted and established in love, may have power, together with all saints, to grasp how wide and long and high and deep is the love of Christ, and to know this love that surpasses knowledge—that you may be filled to the measure of all the fullness of God.* Ephesians 3:17-19 NIV

In Deed

Look for ways that you can be a blessing to others today. Don't wait to be asked to help somebody. Be aware of those in need. Volunteer. Serve. And listen for God's direction in your life.

Sharon Rigsby

53
Loving Hailey

Those whom I love I rebuke and discipline.
Revelation 3:19a NIV

The most memorable job I had in college was the short time I was
a nanny to ten-year-old Hailey. Hailey's family lived in one of the
nicest neighborhoods in Huntsville and had a beautiful home right on
the golf course. Her father was a basketball coach at the university,
and her mother was a flight attendant. They seemed to find success
juggling their demanding schedules, but the two were seldom home
at the same time.

They warned me up front that Hailey was a challenging child, and I
learned within the first week just how challenging she could be. She
refused to do her homework, ran away from me in public, never
picked up after herself, and used extremely foul language. I had
never met a ten-year-old who behaved so badly.

One afternoon during a particularly defiant moment, Hailey stripped
off all of her clothes and ran out the back door and onto the golf
course screaming, "You can't catch me!" while I frantically tried to
chase her down. She headed straight for a bewildered foursome who
looked as if they wanted to help; but because of the awkwardness of
the situation, they just stood there frozen instead.

When I relayed the event to her father that evening, he just shook his head and said, "Hailey will be Hailey" in that same sing-song voice that others use when saying, "Boys will be boys."

The next time I watched Hailey, she had another moment of rebellion and proceeded to hit, kick and scratch me while calling me horrible names I'd never been called before. Then her tantrum erupted into a moment of climax as she grabbed my arm and bit me. Hard. In the split second that followed, I mentally ran down every tip and guideline I'd learned from Hailey's parents and my education professors about dealing with difficult children, and then decided to do the exact opposite.

I bit her back.

Obviously, it wasn't a real bite. There was little to no pressure and no lingering teeth imprints on her arm. It was just enough to get her attention and let her know that there would be consequences if she ever bit me again. But something strange happened in that moment after I retaliated – Hailey smiled. It wasn't there for long, but before she exploded into another string of expletives, she actually smiled. And after the tantrum was over, we enjoyed the most pleasant time together that we'd ever shared.

I could tell that Hailey and I had reached a significant milestone in our relationship; and while we still had a long way to go before she would be a well-behaved child, I knew that she finally understood, and on some level respected, the authority I had over her.

Unfortunately, we never got to explore that relationship more. After hearing the story from both of us that night, Hailey's father politely gave me my last paycheck and told me he would make other arrangements for her care. I'll never forget what he said as I was leaving. "I just don't think you love Hailey like we do."

I didn't *love* her? I wanted to argue that loving Hailey meant giving her rules and consequences for her actions. Loving Hailey meant disciplining Hailey, and from what I'd seen, that was the kind of love she was longing for. But instead, I kept my mouth shut. Then I thanked him for the opportunity, gave Hailey a hug good-bye, and spent the next fifteen years wondering whatever became of her.

It's never fun to be on the receiving end of discipline, but it's also hard to be on the giving end as well. Any parent who's ever found himself saying, "This is going to hurt me more than it hurts you," understands the dilemma. There is a part of you that wants to skip over the punishment phase of your child's rebellion and jump straight to the part where the lesson has been learned and the behavior has been corrected.

But the Bible is clear that to love someone is to discipline him. And if that feels unpleasant for a parent, imagine how God feels when He has to discipline us. But He does it anyway because He loves us. And His discipline has a very specific purpose – it leads to our holiness.

Perhaps you're in the middle of a difficult time right now, and you're wondering why God doesn't just help you skip over it. Could it be that your trials are the result of some poor choices and that God is merely letting you face the consequences of your actions? If so, know that He is more concerned with your holiness than anything else, and that the discipline you are going through is a reflection of His love for you.

In Thought
"Dear Lord, thank You for loving me enough to discipline me. Help me obey Your commands, learn from my mistakes, and embrace Your spiritual "spankings" as stepping stones on the road to holiness. Amen."

In Word

- *Joyful are those you discipline, Lord, those you teach with your instructions.* Psalm 94:12 NLT
- *My child, don't reject the Lord's discipline, and don't be upset when he corrects you. For the Lord corrects those he loves, just as a father corrects a child in whom he delights.* Proverbs 3:11-12 NLT
- *Our fathers disciplined us for a little while as they thought best; but God disciplines us for our good, that we may share in his holiness. No discipline seems pleasant at the time, but painful. Later on, however, it produces a harvest of righteousness and peace for those who have been trained by it.* Hebrews 12:10-11 NIV

In Deed

Resist the urge to ask God for immunity from discipline. Instead, ask Him to show you everything He wants you to learn while you're being disciplined.

Emily Ryan

54
Cast Your Cares Upon Him

Humble yourselves therefore under the mighty hand of God that He may exalt you in due time, casting all your care upon Him for He careth for you.
1 Peter 5: 6-7 KJV

Several years ago I found myself a newlywed looking forward with all the fervor and dreams of any newlywed. I could see a happy home filled with children and laughter . . . But then suddenly, in one moment, that all changed.

My husband was out of town and I awoke ill. I drove myself to the local hospital where I was triaged in the emergency room. My husband's secretary had contacted him and he was on his way. Before he could get there, I was in surgery. It was a surgery that would change my life forever.

I awoke to the rough hands of someone shaking me awake shouting that everything was gone... gone... no more babies. As I slid into the darkness, I felt hot tears slip from my closed eyes. The card on the breakfast tray announced merrily "Happy Mother's Day!"

Years of grief later, I emerged from the shower after work. My face was red and swollen as usual. I stared at the stranger in the mirror and my heart broke again and I began to pray. "God," I begged. "I can't take this pain any more! Please, please, Father, take it from me and give me peace!"

A warmth flooded me and the tears ceased. I was literally filled with a peace I could not understand.

But God wasn't finished.

The next morning we received a call from an older woman who asked for me. She said, "My daughter just had a baby girl and has decided to give her up for adoption. We understand that you might be interested. Will you meet us at the hospital?"

Stunned, I agreed, and the next day we brought home a beautiful baby girl. We thought she was the caboose, but God knew better. Four years later, out of the blue, came our infant son.

Trust God in all things. He truly does care for you. He looks down the years and knows what is best for us and those whose lives we affect. He knew those children would need a home. He also knew that if I could have had children of my own, I wouldn't have considered adoption. God blesses us in ways beyond our understanding.

Often, it is when we are in our darkest hour that we will reach out to the Father the most. Through pain we grow in faith. During times when you are in those deep, dark places, take your pain to Him. Even if you do not have the words, take your thoughts and feelings to Jesus. Lay them at his nail-scarred feet and He will lift you up. In doing so, others will see what giving everything up to Him can truly do. What a fabulous thing to be able to share with the world.

In Thought

"Father, please give me grace to show others what You have taught me through my grief. Let me praise You at all times, through the valleys and on the mountain top. Amen."

In Word

Let us therefore come boldly unto the throne of grace, that we may obtain mercy, and find grace to help in time of need. Hebrews 4:16 KJV

In Deed

- The next time you are around a small child and his parents, observe how that child responds to his parents' love, affection and even discipline. Does he trust his mother? Does he imitate his father? When he doesn't know where the parent is going, does he still follow?
- Use those observations to consider how you can trust God with childlike faith even when you don't understand His ways.

Donna Tovander

55

Meeting Jesus, The Healer

But Peter said, "I do not possess silver and gold, but what I do have I give to you: In the name of Jesus Christ, the Nazarene—walk!"
Acts 3:6 NASB

When I was younger, I received a life-altering injury. Suddenly, I could not walk and, like the beggar at the gate of the temple called Beautiful, I was reaching out for something. I stretched my hands out initially to doctors, friends and family, but I forgot about taking the hand of the only One who truly heals—Jesus Christ. I spent my days in despair after the doctors informed me that I would probably have to use an assistive device, either a walker or wheelchair, for the rest of my life. My despair grew as those around me seemed indifferent to my plight. Finally, in my desperation, I turned to God, but my prayers lacked power, conviction and belief.

Then one day, I met Jesus the Healer. I was sitting outside in the sun bemoaning my fate. I was certain I didn't want to be crippled all of my life or have to depend upon others for my care, but Christ came in the midst of my despair and asked, "What do you really want?"

"I want to be free," I cried and promised that if I could just walk again I'd stand firm all the days of my life. Well, after months of agonizing therapy treatments, I was back on my feet. My doctors were amazed.

They could not understand my transformation, but I did. I prayed with conviction, faith, trust and the belief that God could heal me and He did. My body was whole again!

But this was just the beginning. There was dissension within my family. Now, God called upon me to be the one to stand firm in my faith and follow where He led. He healed me of old anger, pain and unforgiveness. He refused to allow me the comfort of old thoughts, behaviors or convictions. He truly healed me in ways I could not have imagined. I saw a tremendous change in myself, my family and my faith after God healed me. But would I have changed without the healing of my body? I believe God healed me so that I would have a testimony. He may choose not to heal others so that their testimony will be greater, richer and fuller than my own.

Many of us are in need of healing – physical, mental and emotional – and look for it solely through doctors and medicine. But without Christ at the center of our lives, we miss out on the most important healing of all – the healing of our spirits. It is this healing that is most important because our bodies are perishable, but our spirits, once returned to right standing with God, become imperishable. "And inasmuch as it is appointed for men to die once and after this comes judgment, so Christ also, having been offered once to bear the sins of many, will appear a second time for salvation without reference to sin, to those who eagerly await Him" (Hebrews 9:27-28 NASB). God has a purpose for every situation in our lives if we walk with Him in faith believing that He is in control!

Are you in need of healing today? Perhaps, your body is ill or maybe you are suffering in other areas of your life. Trust Him to shelter you, strengthen you and equip you for whatever may lie ahead. Remember, we are created by God for His purposes, not our own. We know we are called to share in the fellowship of Christ's suffering. But we also know that He is with us always no matter what we are called upon to endure because He is faithful, loving and just.

In Thought

"Dear Lord Jesus, I call upon You for healing in my life. But Savior, I am first and foremost Your servant and whatever You call upon me to endure, I know You will give me the grace and strength to endure it. I don't know what form Your healing will take, but Lord I thank You for giving me healing of the spirit – a return to oneness with You and the Father through the Holy Spirit. I ask that Your will be done in my life and I give thanks for You and Your unending gift of love, mercy and grace. Amen."

In Word

- *Heal me, O LORD, and I will be healed; save me and I will be saved, For You are my praise.* Jeremiah 17:14 NASB
- *Don't be impressed with your own wisdom. Instead, fear the Lord and turn away from evil. Then you will have healing for your body and strength for your bones.* Proverbs 3:7-8 NLT
- *Confess your sins to each other and pray for each other so that you may be healed. The earnest prayer of a righteous person has great power and produces wonderful results.* James 5:16 NLT

In Deed

- Go to your local church library and check out *Joni – An Unforgettable Story*, the autobiography of quadriplegic Joni Eareckson Tada.
- For the next week, instead of praying for physical healing for yourself or someone close to you, pray that God will be glorified through the situation.

Patricia Dixon

56
The Hippie's Sister

And we all, who with unveiled faces contemplate the Lord's glory, are being transformed into his image with ever-increasing glory, which comes from the Lord, who is the Spirit.
2 Corinthians 3:18 NIV

My brother, Bruce, was the only hippie in the family, including the extended families of both my mom and dad. He is 8 ½ years older than I, and we adored each other! When I was a baby, he took me to school for "Show and Tell." And as we grew up, he gave me rides in his Triumph convertible with my friends, told me I was prettier when I didn't put "Sun-In" (remember that?) in my hair, and still hugs and kisses me when we see each other.

In fact, because Bruce was born in Austin, Texas, he was rather disturbed that I was born in Michigan and was not a Texan. He actually wrote to Texas Governor John Connally explaining his concern, and the governor sent back a signed certificate declaring me an honorary Texan!

When I was in the fourth grade, we were given the writing assignment: "When I Grow Up." Part of my essay went something like this: "When I grow up, I want a boyfriend with long hair who wears leather fringe vests, beads and flip flops. I want to be a waitress and drive a red

Mustang convertible." Where that waitress ambition came from, I have no idea. But it's easy to see where the other desires came from. I wanted someone like my brother and a car that was cool like his. He was my hero, and I patterned my dreams after the person I loved.

Now, if you know my husband, you know I did not end up with a hippie, even if his hair was a little long when we met. I'm still waiting for the convertible, and it's hard to come by a fringe leather vest these days! But I did marry someone with a great sense of humor, intelligence, and a love for children – qualities that both my brother and my dad had. I think we tend to be drawn to those who emulate the good qualities of those we love.

But above all other role models, God gave us the perfect role model to emulate – Jesus. And through His death on the cross and His resurrection, we are offered a salvation that brings with it His qualities. We are to emulate *Him* above all others!

Who do you want to be when you "grow up?" Do you strive to be like those around you, or do you strive to be like Christ? If we keep Him at the forefront of our adoration and emulate Him in all we do, when others look at us, they should be able to say, "Oh, I know who her Father is!" because they see a family resemblance!

In Thought

"Lord, thank You for giving me a holy legacy to live out. Thank You that You fully accept and love me and want Your good things for me. Please fill me with Your Spirit so that the old me is no longer recognizable, and all that is left is a child who resembles You! Amen."

193

In Word

- *Therefore, as God's chosen people, holy and dearly loved, clothe yourselves with compassion, kindness, humility, gentleness and patience.* Colossians 3:12 NIV
- *By this all will know that you are My disciples, if you have love for one another.* John 13:35 NKJV
- *In the same way, let your light shine before others, that they may see your good deeds and glorify your Father in heaven.* Matthew 5:16 NIV

In Deed

Go through Scripture and list all the qualities of God the Father, Jesus Christ, and the Holy Spirit. Write these on index cards and focus on a different quality each day until you have gone through them all. Pray for His strength as you develop each quality.

Kim Lindquist

Week 8 Notes

_____

_____

_____

_____

_____

_____

_____

_____

_____

_____

_____

_____

_____

_____

_____

57
The
Vegas Syndrome

Since, then, you have been raised with Christ, set your hearts on things above, where Christ is seated at the right hand of God. Set your minds on things above, not on earthly things.
Colossians 3:1-2 NIV

Several years ago, I went with a group of friends to Las Vegas, Nevada, for a wedding. Although we weren't thrilled about the casinos or "night life" that are typical of the city, there were several other aspects of the town we couldn't wait to explore – the lights, the food, the hotels...the lack of humidity! We wanted to experience it all!

We had a great time walking down the streets of Vegas, with perfect hair and six cameras among the four of us, and spent the days going from one hotel to another gawking at the sights. Where else can you experience New York City, the pyramids of Egypt, Caesar's Palace, and Paris, France, all in one day?

However, it was while we were in Paris (that is the Paris Las Vegas Resort) that I had an epiphany. We were standing at the base of the Eiffel Tower attempting to read all the signs that were written *en Français*, when we noticed a sign that beckoned us to pay $15 to go up to the top of the Eiffel Tower. *Why not?* we thought. We'd already had our French baguettes and a little café au lait and besides, when would we ever get such an opportunity? We were in line and poised with our money and cameras when it hit me.

"You know," I said to my friends, "we're not really in Paris." They paused. "And this isn't the real Eiffel Tower." They realized it, too. We had become so caught up in the fanfare and excitement of the city that we forgot that it wasn't the real thing. We may have visited the New York, New York Hotel that day, but we were never really in New York City. And we may have walked through the Excalibur Hotel, but not once were we really in a medieval castle. We had fallen victim to the Vegas Syndrome.

The Vegas Syndrome is one of Satan's greatest tricks, and it is amazing how often we fall for it. He uses anything he can think of – busy calendars, work obligations, family relationships, money challenges – to distract us from the Real Thing (Jesus!) and to lure us into a world in which we forget that silly things like new cars, media rooms, or the latest business deals really don't matter into eternity. We forget that we have a heavenly home and that everything in this world is a small-scale, fleeting illusion of what is to come.

I've yet to make it to the real Eiffel Tower in Paris, but I've heard the view is amazing. And I've yet to make it to my heavenly home, but from what I've read, it will be a place beyond words! We forget that this world – the right here, right now – is Satan's world. It's the cheap, Vegas knockoff, if you will. Our home is in heaven, and to fall short of such a viewpoint is to settle for second best. Let us not spend our lives striving to get to the top of a fake Eiffel Tower!

In Thought

"Dear Lord, please forgive me for the times when I've put so much value on things that are so fleeting. I'll admit I get caught up in the fanfare of the world, and I often forget that You died on the cross to give us so much more! Keep me from being distracted. And in the midst of my everyday life, give me Your eyes to see the things that will truly matter on an eternal level. Then grant me the wisdom and passion to invest in those things. Amen."

In Word

- *But our citizenship is in heaven. And we eagerly await a Savior from there, the Lord Jesus Christ, who, by the power that enables him to bring everything under his control, will transform our lowly bodies so that they will be like his glorious body.* Philippians 3:20-21 NIV

- *Do not love the world or anything in the world. If anyone loves the world, the love of the Father is not in him...The world and its desires pass away, but the man who does the will of God lives forever.* 1 John 2:15 & 17 NIV

In Deed

- Make a list of the things you worry about, the accomplishments you have achieved, or the goals you've set. Then go beside each item and categorize it as "temporary" or "eternal."

- If you sense you might struggle with superficial things, make plans to volunteer at a hospital, feed the homeless, or go on a mission trip. When we're exposed to struggles outside our little bubbles, it's often easier to gain an eternal perspective on life.

Emily Ryan

58
One Please

---

*My flesh and my heart may fail, but God is the strength
of my heart and my portion forever.*
Psalm 73:26 NIV

A man walked slowly down the long road toward the port gate.
However, he wasn't carrying any luggage. Most people coming
toward the gate had lots of luggage preparing to make a long trip to
visit family and friends in faraway places. The man walked right up
to the distributor and said, "One packet, please." He actually asked
for one in a specific language. No further words were spoken. The
distributor handed the man the packet and watched in amazement as
he took it, turned around, and walked back the way he had come. But
now he had a New Testament in his own language in his hand.

These packets contain a New Testament and some other materials
and are distributed by volunteers to people in different languages all
over the world. As you might imagine, not everyone readily accepts
a packet. We make it very clear what the packets contain because
we are not ashamed of the Gospel. Sometimes volunteers can get
discouraged on days when they have offered packets to many people
and have had very few accept one. It is at such times that we must
remember that what we do is for Him, not us, and we are to persevere.
God will direct the packets. He wants our faithfulness and willingness
to serve Him. On other days many will readily take the packets and
we trust the Lord to know where He plans for His Word to end up. We
are the literal physical deliverer of the Word at that moment. The Holy

Spirit takes over from there.

We are fortunate to live in a country where many households own at least three or four Bibles, but that is not the case everywhere. It is our responsibility and our privilege to do everything we can to get God's Word into the homes and hearts of those who do not have easy access to it. If our hearts are open to the Lord's calling to serve Him, He will give us all we need to complete the task of distributing His Word to others. All we must do is be ready to be used by Him.

In Thought
"Lord, thank You for Your Word and the opportunities we have to share it with others all over the world. I pray many will come to know Jesus as Savior through these efforts. Amen."

In Word
- *All over the world this gospel is producing fruit and growing, just as it has been doing among you since the day you heard it and understood God's grace in all its truth.* Colossians 1:6 NIV
- *The Lord will fulfill his purpose for me; your love, O Lord, endures forever—do not abandon the works of your hands.* Psalm 138:8 NIV
- *For God did not give us a spirit of timidity, but a spirit of power, of love, and of self-discipline.* 2 Timothy 1:7 NIV

In Deed
- Go to your local Christian bookstore and purchase 5-10 small copies of the New Testament to keep in your car.
- Go through the Bibles and highlight a few verses: John 3:16 and the verses in the "Roman Road" – Romans 3:23, 6:23, 5:8, and 10:9-10.
- When you sense the Lord prompting you to give someone a Bible, do so immediately and pray that His Word falls on soft hearts.

Sharon Rigsby

59

The Beetle That Went Up a Hill and Came Down a Mountain

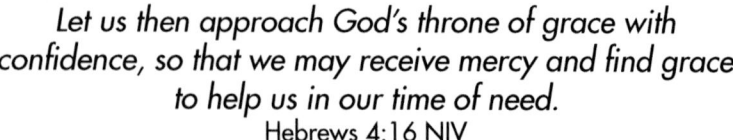

Let us then approach God's throne of grace with confidence, so that we may receive mercy and find grace to help us in our time of need.
Hebrews 4:16 NIV

I'll never forget learning to drive a standard, a.k.a. a stick-shift. It was a gray, VW Beetle, one of the great icons of the 1970's! I was about 15 or so and my childhood friend, Linda, who was like my older sister, was my instructor. I felt proud and privileged that she would take the time to teach me…and I was nervous!

For those who remember, the main goal is learning not to stall (especially in an intersection) and not to grind the gears! I did a little of both. But the highlight of the day was when I finally got the hang of it! I was getting smoother with the gears and gliding along when a car came from the opposite direction.

I did what any responsible driver would do upon realizing he or she was going the wrong way on a one-way street. I panicked! Then I quickly drove up an incline of a nearby business. Thankfully, we were on a road "less traveled" and nobody was put at risk.

As we laughed with relief, I didn't yet realize I had cruised out of the proverbial frying pan and was now in the fire.

My challenge now was to get *off* of the incline without rolling back into oncoming traffic. I can't tell you how many times I stalled that poor "bug" out. When I'd let off the clutch to give it enough gas to go back, I just wasn't quick enough on the gas. I was literally stuck!

Putting the hand brake on, I switched seats with Linda so she could get us off of this hill. I can't imagine how long I might have been there on that concrete mountain if left to my own devices!

So many times in our lives we must plead a "learning curve" as the Lord teaches us something new, leads us to a new venture, guides us to a new ministry, gives us a new relationship, allows us to be parents, etc. Just when we get "the hang of it," we may realize that we, too, are going the "wrong way." Maybe it's a decision we made. Maybe it's the fact that we have taken on too much at once. Or maybe we are working in the flesh rather than seeking the Lord in the details and then moving on His leading.

We may feel "stuck" during these times and need the godly guidance of a brother or sister in Christ to help us get back on track. Pride has no place in this scenario; but humility, in both the "stuckee" and the one assisting, is a must. And godly counsel will always line up with the Word and with what God has revealed to us. God, of course, does not always answer in our time frame. But we know one thing for sure – when we are doing things that line up with His will and His ways, we should have His peace with us.

Above all other helpers, the Lord Jesus sent to us the ultimate Helper, His Holy Spirit (see John 14:15-27). The best thing we can do during times of feeling overwhelmed, discouraged, confused or frustrated is to put on the brake, move over, and let Him do the driving!

In Thought

"Dear Lord, thank You for being an ever present help in times of trouble. Thank You, also, that You have given me Your family to share in my ups and downs. Help me to be humble enough to seek Your guidance as well as the advice of godly brothers and sisters. Thank You that You are in charge of my life, in big things and small. Amen."

In Word

- But you, LORD, do not be far from me. You are my strength; come quickly to help me. Psalm 22:19 NIV
- Likewise the Spirit also helps in our weaknesses. For we do not know what we should pray for as we ought, but the Spirit Himself makes intercession for us with groanings which cannot be uttered. Romans 8:26 NKJV

In Deed

If you are feeling frustrated today, spend some time in prayer regarding what is bothering you. Ask the Lord to reveal to you through His word His next step for you. Also ask the Lord to encourage you through the godly counsel of a brother or sister. Remain in regular prayer and spend time in the Word to better hear His leading.

Kim Lindquist

60
The Truth About Lying

The man of integrity walks securely, but he who takes crooked paths will be found out.
Proverbs 10:9 NIV

When I was young, I went with my friend and her mother to the grocery store. We spent some time in the floral department where my friend's mom picked out a small plant to buy. Then she searched through the decorative pots until she found one that was a perfect fit for the plant. "Does this look nice?" she asked, and we both assured her it was fine.

When it came time to check out, the plant was still in the pot, so the cashier rang up the two items as one. My friend stepped in to correct her mistake. "I think those are two separate things," she said, and the cashier thanked her for her honesty and rang up the items individually.

My friend's mom smiled as if she was proud of her daughter's integrity, but when we got to the car, it was a completely different story. "How could you do something so stupid?" she yelled at my friend. "We would have gotten that plant for free if you hadn't opened your big mouth and told her they were priced separately! I should make you pay it out of your own money so next time you'll think before you speak!"

I was dumbfounded. I'd never seen this woman so angry before, and I couldn't believe she was actually mad at my friend for being honest. Until then, I thought everyone tried to be truthful – especially adults.

But unfortunately, I've found this type of deception to be even more prevalent now that I've grown up. People who have already graduated from college still use their student IDs to get discounted movie tickets. Parents lie about their children's ages to avoid paying for their meals at restaurants. Business owners save receipts for personal expenses in order to write them off on their taxes. Small and seemingly "innocent" lies show up so often that most have come to tolerate them and shrug them off as something everyone does anyway.

The Bible says that the devil is the "father of lies" and that when he lies, he "speaks his native language" (John 8:44 NIV). Most of us don't consider ourselves to be liars about the "big" things in life. We are faithful to our spouses. We don't shoplift. We don't cheat in school. But when it comes to the "little" things, the temptation to fudge the truth is one we face every day, and sometimes, our half-truths and omitted facts seem so insignificant, we don't even realize that it's equivalent to lying.

As Christians, we're to be honest in each and every circumstance – those that are in public, those that are in private, those that seem "big," and those that seem "small." "Truthful lips endure forever, but a lying tongue lasts only a moment" (Proverbs 12:19 NIV). Are honesty and integrity among the virtues for which you're known by those close to you? What about by God? Does He, who sees all and knows all, also see the truth in you?

If we are being honest, many of us would have to say, probably not.

In Thought

"Dear Lord, please forgive me for the times I've been dishonest. I pray that You would open my eyes to the "little white lies" that creep from my lips when I don't even realize it, and I pray You would help me speak the truth and conduct myself with integrity at all times. Amen."

In Word

- *These are the things you are to do: Speak the truth to each other, and render true and sound judgment in your courts.* Zechariah 8:16 NIV
- *You belong to your father, the devil, and you want to carry out your father's desire. He was a murderer from the beginning, not holding to the truth, for there is no truth in him. When he lies, he speaks his native language, for he is a liar and the father of lies.* John 8:44 NIV
- *Honest scales and balances are from the LORD; all the weights in the bag are of his making.* Proverbs 16:11 NIV
- *Buy the truth and do not sell it; get wisdom, discipline and understanding.* Proverbs 23:23 NIV

In Deed

The next time you find yourself saying something that isn't 100% truthful, rather than sweep it under the rug, go back and make it right.

Emily Ryan

61
Rotting Bones

Let the LORD's people show him reverence, for those who honor him will have all they need. Even strong young lions sometimes go hungry, but those who trust in the LORD will never lack any good thing.
Psalm 34:9-10 NLT

As I look around me, I see cracks in my ceiling and floors, and we have a busted pipe underground that is connected to the washing machine causing us to have to run the hose outside the back door when we want to do laundry. We have only one working shower and water comes in from under the slab in the living room when it rains heavy. We also have a hole over the fireplace because the roof needs to be replaced. As I look around, I only get overwhelmed at the shape this house is in; but we are renters, and I long for us to be able to purchase a home of our own this year.

Recently, many of my family members have bought new houses, started new jobs or purchased nice new vehicles. Some have parents who have helped furnish their homes and still sometimes give them monthly allowances as well. I see this and I get discouraged. I see them prosper while we struggle and the things around us fall apart. Yes, I get envious at times. The definition of envy is jealousy, resentment aroused by another's advantage or possessions. In James 3:14-15 NIV we are told, "But if you harbor bitter envy and selfish ambition in your hearts, do not boast about it or deny the truth. Such 'wisdom' does not come down from heaven but is earthly, unspiritual, of the devil."

I serve a great and mighty God who has always provided for me what I need, not what I always want. I must remain steadfast in knowing that I would much rather serve Him than feed my selfish desires, and that I want to see the things I do have as blessings from God. I do not want to become bitter inside and always wish for the "greener pasture." I want to remain humble and faithful to the One who will make me prosper in my eternal home in heaven.

As I long to have what they have, I also realize that I have something they don't – a relationship with Christ. I wouldn't trade that for anything, and it is my job to make sure they have eternal riches that far exceed the ones they have here on earth. I must remain focused on my purpose in living for Him and not be concerned about the possessions they have that are greater than mine. "A heart of peace gives life to the body, but envy rots the bones" (Proverbs 14:30 NIV).

In Thought

"Oh Lord, please help to keep my focus on what is the most important thing in this world: You. Let my eyes not stray to earthly possessions and ways other family members are prospering, but remind me that You will always provide what we need and that You do bless us with the desires of our heart. You give us only what we can handle, and let me remember that. Thank You for what I do have and the many blessings You show me daily. I ask this in Your most amazing grace. Amen."

In Word

- *God has made everything beautiful for its own time. He has planted eternity in the human heart, but even so, people cannot see the whole scope of God's work from beginning to end.* Ecclesiastes 3:11 NLT
- *Enjoy what you have rather than desiring what you don't have. Just dreaming about nice things is meaningless; it is like chasing the wind.* Ecclesiastes 6:0 NLT
- *Stay away from the love of money; be satisfied with what you have. For God has said, "I will never fail you. I will never forsake you."* Hebrews 13:5 NLT

In Deed

- Next time you find yourself desiring to have the better of things that someone else has, focus in closer to home and start counting your blessings instead. You will then get back on track as to who provides for you what you need.
- Meditate on God's promises that He will never leave you nor forsake you and that the things of this earth are only temporary. You can't take them with you when you go.

Cindy Cañas

62
Understanding Amazing Grace

And He said to me, "My grace is sufficient for you, for power is perfected in weakness." Most gladly, therefore, I will rather boast about my weaknesses, so that the power of Christ may dwell in me.
2 Corinthians 12:9 NASB

I didn't understand grace until I looked it up in the dictionary. It is defined as "special favor" and "unmerited divine assistance." I knew God loved me and I knew I had been helped in situations throughout my life as a Christian, but grace still eluded me. Why would God, after everything He had already done for me in sending Christ to die for me, grant me anything more? Then, I realized it had nothing to do with who I was, but everything to do with who God is! It is His nature to be loving, merciful and giving to His children. He continues to bring instances of grace into our lives because it in is His very nature to do so.

About a year ago, I began writing a book of poetry. All of the poetry in the book was for and about God. I titled it *Praise is What I Do* because I was pouring my heart out to God. It is usually difficult to get a book of poetry published, and several people in the publishing industry told me it would be difficult, if not impossible, to get mine published. However, I continued to write as I would for publication and even took pictures for the front and back covers. I was just starting to look for publishing opportunities when a publisher called me. I was skeptical at first because I had never heard of a publisher calling someone to ask for a meeting, but I prayed and sent him an excerpt of my book. As it turned out, someone who knew my sister worked for this publisher and recommended that he contact me. As a result of this "unmerited favor," my book is now published!

Recently, a Christian friend who had worked for NASA became unemployed. Suddenly, she was presented with, not one, but two really good job opportunities. She finally accepted a great job at Johns Hopkins University. They also paid all of her relocation expenses, reimbursed her for travel into the area to find an apartment and are doing everything they can to make her transition into her new position a success! Here we have another example of God's grace.

Who are we that God takes such care of us? We have received God's "unmerited divine assistance" and "special favor" because we are called according to His purposes and are walking by faith, not sight. "Now to him who is able to do immeasurably more than all we ask or imagine, according to his power that is at work within us, to him be glory in the church and in Christ Jesus throughout all generations, for ever and ever! Amen" (Ephesians 3:20-21 NIV).

Our God is so faithful to His nature and His promises, and He has an abundance of grace just waiting to be poured out in the lives of His children. Perhaps He has already blessed you so abundantly that you are overlooking His grace and calling it coincidence. Maybe, you are being blessed and are taking it for granted. Don't belittle God's blessings by explaining them away. Receive them. Acknowledge them. Then praise God for them!

In Thought

"Dear Lord, thank You for Your unending and amazing grace. You have blessed me in so many ways, I could never acknowledge them all. I pray that You would keep Your hand of blessing upon my life and that You would keep my eyes open to the evidences of grace that surround me on a daily basis. Amen."

In Word

- *If you, then, though you are evil, know how to give good gifts to your children, how much more will your Father in heaven give good gifts to those who ask him!* Matthew 7:11 NIV
- *The Word became flesh and made his dwelling among us. We have seen his glory, the glory of the one and only Son, who came from the Father, full of grace and truth.* John 1:14 NIV

In Deed

- The next time you sit down to pray, spend time praising God for all of your blessings instead of petitioning Him for more.
- Let this "attitude of gratitude" spill over into every area of your life. Say thank you to everyone from your family members to those who wait on you in restaurants.
- Finally, make praise a part of your daily conversation with God. Praise Him for everything. He deserves it!

Patricia Dixon

213

63
The Bunny Chauffeur

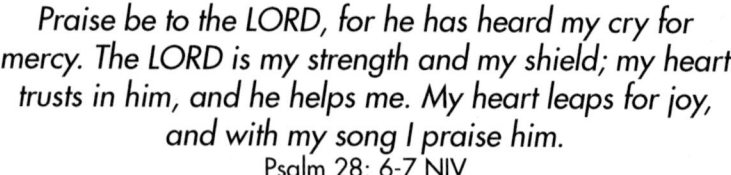

Praise be to the LORD, for he has heard my cry for mercy. The LORD is my strength and my shield; my heart trusts in him, and he helps me. My heart leaps for joy, and with my song I praise him.
Psalm 28: 6-7 NIV

My favorite television show is exactly the same as it has been since I was eleven years old. "America's Funniest Home Videos" is a reality television show on ABC which usually airs really funny home videos. Now, twenty years later, I still find myself loving to watch the slapstick, physical comedy of unsuspecting people falling down, getting hit by something, or just saying very embarrassing things! Of all those hundreds of shows I have seen over the years, my all-time favorite is a short clip of a dog and a bunny rabbit.

The voice of the host begins by saying, "There's nothing lower in life than being a bunny chauffeur!" Then, out of a house races a small dog pulling a little wagon with a bunny as its passenger! The nervous bunny sits perilously in the wagon with his ears straight back in horror. The dog continues racing around the corner and then down the street at break-neck speeds. The bunny's only movement is a quick balance check as he keeps himself from tumbling out of the wagon while he's whipped around a corner. The clip ends as we see the back of the bunny flying down the sidewalk with no end in sight! I have seen this video so many times, but it still makes me laugh out loud. I guess I can relate to how that bunny must feel, as life so often takes us on unexpected and wild rides!

Events in our lives can affect us just like that dog who ran with abandonment, giving no consideration to his terrified passenger in the wagon. So many things are out of our control, and we find ourselves like the bunny, just hanging on and hoping to stay aboard! As Christians, we still do not have control over many aspects of our lives, but instead have placed our confidence in a Savior who has it all under control. We can be confident that we are in His care. Our goal is not to survive each of life's unexpected turns but to experience joy in all circumstances. But the only way we can experience this joy is to be rooted in the fact that God is in control of everything in our lives…whether things seem slow and easy or they're racing at break-neck speeds!

In Thought
"Lord, praise be to You, the Alpha and Omega. You are my strength and my shield. Teach me to trust in You no matter what circumstances arise. Fill me with Your joy and peace so that I may overflow with hope by the power of the Holy Spirit. Amen."

In Word
- *May the God of hope fill you with all joy and peace as you trust in him, so that you may overflow with hope by the power of the Holy Spirit.* Romans 15:13 NIV
- *"For I know the plans I have for you," declares the LORD, "plans to prosper you and not to harm you, plans to give you hope and a future. Then you will call on me and come and pray to me, and I will listen to you."* Jeremiah 29:11-12 NIV

215

In Deed

- Make a list of times when your life became difficult. Next to those instances record what your action was to remedy the problem. Finally, record how the event or problem was ultimately resolved.
- Notice how many times you turned to the Lord and how many times you dealt with the problem in your own strength. Resolve to relinquish control to the Lord *first* the next time you face a difficult situation.

Mikelle Challenger

Week 9 Notes

64
Sunday Morning Blowout

Near the cross of Jesus stood his mother...When Jesus saw his mother there, and the disciple whom he loved standing nearby, he said to her, "Woman, here is your son," and to the disciple, "Here is your mother." From that time on, this disciple took her into his home.
John 19:25-27 NIV

I seldom see people I know as I drive on the freeway, but one particular Sunday morning, I recognized a good friend as I drove to church. I honked and waved as I drove past her and thought it nothing more than a fun coincidence since we were both headed to the same place.

Several minutes later, as I reached the top of a very high overpass, my car hit a large piece of road debris and one of my tires immediately went flat. Suddenly, I was stranded several hundred feet up and right in the middle of a potentially dangerous section of freeway just minutes short of my destination.

I was able to pull over to a relatively safe area, but my mind reeled at how I was going to manage to walk all the way down the off ramp in traffic with two small children, a diaper bag, a purse, and my Bible and still make it to church in time to teach my Sunday school class. Plus, of all the days, I'd chosen to wear heels that morning. It did not look promising.

I looked up and could see our church's large, 170-foot cross right in front of me. And in that instant, I remembered my friend and realized that she should be just moments behind me. I looked out my window just in time to see her coming up from the other side of the overpass and flagged her down. Her husband – who "just happens" to work on tires for a living "just happened" to be right behind her in his work truck – was able to change my tire and we were all back on the road in no time at all.

As I parked my van at the foot of the large, white cross on our church campus, I realized that God had provided provisions for my unexpected car trouble before I ever even knew I had a need. Miraculously, I even made it to class in time to teach my Sunday school lesson.

There is a moment in John 19:25-27, while Jesus is suffering on the cross, that often gets overlooked. Since Jesus' earthly father, Joseph, is not mentioned at the crucifixion, it is assumed that he had already passed away. Because His mother, Mary, was a widow, the responsibility of her care and wellbeing fell to Jesus, the eldest son. So when Jesus sees His mother standing at the foot of the cross near John the disciple, He takes the time – in the midst of His pain and His agony – to make sure that His mother will be taken care of after His death. He passes on the responsibility to John and makes certain that both he and Mary know that from then on John is to treat Mary as if she were his own mother and look after her as such.

Even while dying on the cross, Jesus was concerned with meeting needs. He answered prayers before they were ever prayed and arranged provisions before the needs were even exposed.

Sometimes when we tell Him of a circumstance or obstacle that has suddenly come up, we feel as if He was caught off guard just as much as we were. But we forget that He not only knew about our needs before we did, He has also been at work behind the scenes in order to meet those needs in His divine and perfect timing.

In Thought

"Dear Jesus, thank You that You know what I will need even before I do. Before I even express a concern, You are already at work on a resolution. Thank You for Your supernatural provisions, and help me to remember that You are the great Provider the next time a need suddenly catches me by surprise. Amen."

In Word

- *There is no one like the God of Israel. He rides across the heavens to help you, across the skies in majestic splendor.* Deuteronomy 33:26 NLT
- *God is our refuge and strength, always ready to help in times of trouble.* Psalm 46:1 NLT
- *In my distress I called to the LORD; I cried to my God for help. From his temple he heard my voice; my cry came before him, into his ears.* Psalm 18:6 NIV

In Deed

- Make a list of five needs you have had in the past year and how the Lord has met those needs.
- Start a prayer journal listing five needs you have right now. Leave plenty of space to record how and when the Lord meets those needs!
- When you start to feel hopeless, follow some age-old advice: Work like it all depends on you, and pray like it all depends on God.

Emily Ryan

65
What's That Cross Mean, Mommy?

But God demonstrates his own love for us in this: While we were still sinners, Christ died for us.
Romans 5:8 NIV

As a parent of two young boys, I find that there is a fine line to walk between telling them the whole truth and telling them what they need to know at their tender ages. It seems that it is not until you find yourself trying to answer the simple "why" questions of a young child that you truly understand the world around you.

This was true for me the summer of 2009 when our oldest son, James, was two years old. From his car seat, he could see the big white cross that sits on the campus of our church, and he knew that seeing it meant we had almost arrived at our destination. Every time we approached Beltway 8, he would become excited and strain his little neck to see the cross.

On one of those many trips to church, another "why" question came from the back seat. James asked, "What's that cross mean, Mommy?" Even though I knew the question would come eventually, I did not know exactly how much to tell my young toddler. I contemplated how to tell him that the cross is a reminder that our Lord and Savior, Jesus

Christ, hung on a cross and died to save us from our sins. I remember looking at my husband who was also working on his answer. I stumbled around, talking about Jesus and trying to omit any big and scary words. After a few moments, though, I looked back to see him staring even harder at the cross that was getting larger and larger as we neared it. I paused in thought, and again he asked urgently, "But Mommy, what's that cross *mean*?" This time his little finger was pointing at it. I now felt panicked, knowing I did not want to miss this teaching opportunity, and at the same time wanting to make it very clear to him. I felt very frustrated! I had been in church my entire life, so I should be able to answer this simple question from my son! Finally, I blurted out, "James, Honey, it means that Jesus loves you." He smiled, satisfied with the answer.

Now, each time he comes to church and sees the cross he says, "Mommy, Jesus loves you...and me, too!" It is such a simple answer for such a complex subject, but it is the truth! We have crosses to remind us that Jesus paid the ultimate price for all our sins, and His death was the result. Then, He rose from the dead! He died for us because He loves us. One day, I will explain to my boys all of the details that the cross represents: salvation, redemption, justification, grace. But until then, it's enough that they recognize the cross as a symbol of God's love.

No matter how much we the study the Bible, we always come away with the simple truth that God loves us! Whether looking at a beautiful sunset, a newborn baby or a simple cross, we can be reminded of God's perfect and complete love for us. So the next time you find yourself looking at a cross, remember it means that Jesus loves you, too!

In Thought

"Lord, thank You for showing me Your love in so many ways. Thank You for the reminder of the testimony of seeing a cross so that I can rest in the knowledge that You love me. It's a perfect and everlasting love that I do not deserve. Thank You, Lord, for shedding Your precious blood on the cross and paying the price for us all. Amen."

In Word

- *For God so loved the world that he gave his one and only Son, that whoever believes in him shall not perish but have eternal life.* John 3:16 NIV
- *And from Jesus Christ, who is the faithful witness, the firstborn from the dead, and the ruler of the kings of the earth. To him who loves us and has freed us from our sins by his blood.* Revelation 1:5 NIV

In Deed

Crosses show up all around us – on clothing, on jewelry, as decoration, and on buildings. Spend the day paying special attention to all of the crosses you see, and thank God for His love each time you see one.

Mikelle Challenger

66

An Irreplaceable Role

Blessed are they who maintain justice,
who constantly do what is right.
Psalm 106:3 NIV

After nearly thirty years of being out of the jury pool due to motherhood, I was summoned to criminal court. When I scanned the jury summons thoroughly and saw no exemption for home schooling, I groaned about the interruption this would create to my busy life.

On the appointed day I made my appearance, and much to my dismay, I was chosen for the jury. For the next three days, I spent many hours with people I had never met. Before testimony began, we were taken out to lunch together in a nice restaurant escorted by a friendly deputy who grinned and told us, "You're family now."

After the testimony phase of the trial ended the next day, we began deliberations. Eventually, we sent a message to the judge that we were deadlocked 4 to 8. He replied, "Continue." A lunch of sandwiches was served, and I heard the Lord whisper in my ear to pray. I reluctantly obeyed Him and asked my new family, "Does anyone mind if I pray for our food and the deliberations?" To my surprise they all heartily agreed. I decided to make it short and to the point. I asked the Lord for His blessing on us and the food, and that His justice would prevail as we deliberated.

Hours later after much discussion and several votes we were still deadlocked. It was then the judge came to tell us the defendant had accepted a plea bargain. He praised us for our sense of fairness saying he realized the prosecutor had failed to prove her case beyond a reasonable doubt. But he also told us something that couldn't come out in the trial; the defendant was a repeat offender. His attorney had convinced him that eight months in the county jail was infinitely better than the possible two to twenty years in prison he could get if the case was retried.

I was in awe! Our prayer was answered. God's justice had, indeed, prevailed. According to the rules that had been laid out for us, we could not have convicted this man on the evidence presented, yet he received his deserved punishment. I also had the incredible feeling that God had used me to accomplish His purposes. What if I had been one of those four out of five the judge had told us that just ignored their jury summons?

By allowing us to see His justice done using imperfect people in an imperfect system, God gives us a much broader view of what He has designed as our civic duty. Each of us has been cast by our Creator to play an irreplaceable role as we walk this earth. If we refuse to accept it, we change the course of our lives and possibly even the course of history.

In Thought

"God, I acknowledge that Your ways are not my ways. Create in me the desire to seek Your perfect will as I plan my days and make choices that could profoundly affect the course of my life and the lives of those around me. Amen."

In Word

- *"For I know the plans I have for you," says the Lord. "They are plans for good and not for disaster, to give you a future and a hope. In those days when you pray, I will listen. If you look for me wholeheartedly, you will find me."* Jeremiah 29:11-13 NLT
- *You can make many plans, but the Lord's purpose will prevail.* Proverbs 19:21 NLT

In Deed

- If you're not a registered voter, become one today. Then exercise your civic duty and cast an informed and prayerful vote every chance you get.
- Ask God if there are other areas in your community where He would have you become more involved – your local school board, your homeowner's association, or your local city council.

Janie Southard

67
The Great Fishing Day

*"Come, follow me," Jesus said, "and
I will make you fishers of men."*
Matthew 4:19 NIV

When my son, Gideon, was young, he took me "fishing" in his bedroom. The floor became a lake and his bed turned into a boat. The toys on the floor were no longer toys, but crocodiles, and two long, brown wrapping paper tubes became our trusty fishing poles.

I followed his lead into the world of the imaginary and mimicked his motions as he sat on the boat with his fishing pole dangling over the water. Every few moments he'd look at me and smile and then make a comment about how the fish weren't biting yet.

Finally, after a couple of minutes, he suddenly sat up straight and looked at me with eyes as wide as saucers. "Mom, I think I felt something!"

"You did? Well, reel it in so we can see if you caught anything!" He raised his wrapping paper tube/fishing pole high in the air and acted like he was examining his line. "What is it?" I asked, careful not to jump to assumptions.

"It's a great big fish!" he exclaimed, and went right back to fishing after he put his big catch into the boat.

Now that I knew how the game was played, I waited for a bit and pretended to get a nibble on my own line. "Gideon," I whispered, "I think I got something!" He watched quietly as I made a big, dramatic show of reeling in my line and acting as if the fish was so big and heavy that it was hard to reel in. Finally, I held my pole up triumphantly and exclaimed, "Wow! Look! I caught one, too!"

Gideon looked at me, looked at the cardboard tube and said simply, "No, you didn't."

I realized then what it really meant to go "fishing" with my son. It meant that we did the fishing together, but he did all the catching on his own!

Several of Jesus' disciples were fishermen by trade before they left their boats to follow Jesus; and when He first met Peter and Andrew, He told them to follow Him and He would make them "fishers of men." They took this call to evangelism seriously as they shared the good news of the gospel everywhere they went, and it's a call to evangelism we still take to heart even today. We're to share Christ with those around us. We're to give our testimonies often. We're to do everything we can to witness to others and be "fishers of men."

But the one thing we so often forget is that God never tells us to be "catchers" of men at all. He just tells us to fish. The burden of the catch has always been on His shoulders, not ours. Sometimes it can take so much preparation to finally build up enough courage to share Christ with someone that we're disappointed if they don't accept Him on the spot. We think maybe we said the wrong thing or we failed in our efforts. But we never know what's going on in a person's heart like God does. And because of that, all we can do is continue to fish – continue to share Christ whenever we can – and leave the catching up to Him.

In Thought

"Dear God, please help me refrain from keeping score somehow when I share Christ with others. Help me simply to be obedient to the command to be Your witness and not get so caught up in the results that it discourages me from continuing to tell others about You. Thank You that You know the hearts of those around me and that You never expect me to do what only You can – catch those hearts for Your kingdom. Amen."

In Word

- *Then hear from heaven, your dwelling place. Forgive and act; deal with everyone according to all they do, since you know their hearts (for you alone know every human heart).* 1 Kings 8:39 NIV
- *God, who knows the heart, showed that he accepted them by giving the Holy Spirit to them, just as he did to us.* Acts 15:8 NIV

In Deed

Next time you feel the Holy Spirit prompting you to share Christ with someone, do it before you have a chance to analyze the situation. Then, resist the urge to push or nag afterwards, and instead, place all of your follow-up energy on praying that God will "catch" the heart you've been fishing for.

Emily Ryan

68

Michael J. Fox

*Will you never look away from me,
or let me alone even for an instant?*
Job 7:19 NIV

I will never forget my first day of high school. I was so nervous. I remember walking into the new, intimidating building and not seeing one person that I recognized from my junior high. It did not help that all the students around me were greeting friends, making me feel all the more lonely. I picked up my class assignment for the semester and headed for my homeroom, all the while frantically searching for a familiar face. I really did not consider myself an insecure person; but on the first day of something as big as high school, even the most confident kid needs a friend! I felt myself getting frantic as I did not see anyone I even remotely knew in the jammed hallways. Then, as I passed the glass walls of the library, I remember sending up a quick little prayer that went something like, "Lord, please let me see someone I know." At that very moment, I saw someone I recognized, and I instantly reacted by stopping the flow of traffic and turning with a flourished wave saying in a loud voice, "Hi!" I just as suddenly realized that I was looking at a life-size poster of the actor, Michael J. Fox, smiling back at me! I was so humiliated. I looked to see if anyone saw my mistake and was laughing at me. Even though no one seemed to notice, I quickly ducked my head and scrambled to my classroom and found the first available seat. I was fighting away tears when I felt a tap on my shoulder and saw a friend of mine smiling back at me. I knew immediately that God had sent a friend when I needed one the most!

Thankfully, I did manage to find and renew some previous friendships, as well as make many more new friends throughout my four years of high school. But I also learned a very important lesson that day, other than the importance of being more specific in your prayers. I learned that Jesus is the friend that everyone needs. If we are born-again believers, having invited Christ into our lives, He will always be with us, especially when we find ourselves alone and needing to see a familiar face. Ironically, I ended up having to pass by the poster of Michael J. Fox every morning on my way to homeroom, and it reminded me all year that God was with me as well!

In Thought
"Lord, thank You for never leaving me or forsaking me. Even in the deepest valleys and darkest times You are with me. Thank You that I am never truly alone. Amen."

In Word
Even when I walk through the darkest valley, I will not be afraid, for you are close beside me. Your rod and your staff protect and comfort me. Psalm 23:4 NLT

In Deed
- Remember a time in your life when you were truly alone and did not feel you had a friend to call on. Did you call on the Lord during that time? How did He answer your call?
- Pray today and thank Him for being your friend.

Mikelle Challenger

69

Praise

Because Your lovingkindness is better than life,
my lips will praise You.
Psalm 63:3 NASB

I once knew a woman named Susan. Susan was always talking about what she was praying for – usually material things like a new car or a better job. One day, while she was reciting her usual list of expectations from God, I asked her, "Have you ever stopped to thank God for all the things He has already supplied?" Susan looked stunned, opened her mouth to speak, but started weeping instead. Susan's attitude is like that of many people who think of God as an unending supplier who does not want our praise or gratitude for what He has already given us. Many of us think of God with an air of entitlement. However, God owes us nothing! We owe Him everything. It is the height of human foolishness to get our relationship with God so twisted.

How many times a day do we praise God? Do we live with an attitude of gratitude toward God for His plan of salvation for us, or do we accept the gift with a worldly attitude of expectation and entitlement? Keeping an attitude of gratitude is hard for most of us. Most of us struggle to stay upbeat and positive throughout each day. And many of us have developed an attitude of dullness when thinking of God. We know He is there, but because we cannot see Him, we lose the bright excitement and joy we knew upon first coming to faith in Christ. We allow the world to blunt the edge of our conviction and settle into a staid routine of praying to God when it is convenient for us. We pray when we need something or when someone we know or love is sick. Occasionally, we might even remember to thank God for something in passing. Is this your attitude today?

It is not the attitude we should have toward God!

The Bible says in Revelation that the hosts of heaven fell on their faces and worshipped God saying, "Amen, blessing and glory and wisdom and thanksgiving and honor and power and might, be to our God forever and ever. Amen" (7:11-12 NASB). Is this your attitude toward God?

God saved us because of who He is, not because of who we are! He is the Creator, the Holy One, the Alpha and Omega, the Beginning and the End. Because of Christ, we are returned to right standing with God. We become children of God and joint heirs with Jesus Christ.

Can we really grasp the scope of our blessing or the magnitude of the homage we owe to God for His amazing plan of salvation? To fall on our faces and give God the glory He so richly deserves is a pittance compared to what we owe a loving Savior who took our sins upon Himself to pay a debt we owed!

Are you giving God the glory in your life? Examine your life and ask yourself, "Does God have the premier place? Am I giving Him the glory at all times in my life whether my circumstances are good or bad?" If this is not the attitude of your heart, pray for God to forgive you for your unbelief, self-reliance and pride. He is faithful to forgive us and answer our prayers. Resolve to give God everything —all your problems, concerns, trials – then stand and watch Him work.

In Thought

"Dear God, I know You are the Almighty Creator. You created everything and I will have no other gods before You. Not myself, my desires, other people or my circumstances. I know You can handle everything going on in my life, and I praise You for all of my many blessings and for Christ's ultimate display of love on the cross. Amen."

In Word

- *The Lord is my strength and my song; he has given me victory. This is my God, and I will praise him—my father's God, and I will exalt him!* Exodus 15:2 NLT
- *Let everything that has breath praise the LORD. Praise the LORD.* Psalm 150:6 NIV

In Deed

- Spend time each day thanking God for all He has done in your life.
- Make a list of your blessings and post them where you can see them every day. Add items to the list as they occur to you.
- Share with others all the ways in which God has blessed you.
- Make up your own special prayer of praise to God for all He has done for you.

Patricia Dixon

70
The Faith That Enron Built

For where your treasure is, there your heart will be also.
Matthew 6:21 NIV

The best Christmas I've experienced thus far was in December 2001, just after the fall of Enron. Known around the world as one of the most devastating events in the business world, it holds for me precious memories and many lessons in faith.

For days prior to my husband's losing his job, I kept thinking he was just worrying for nothing. Each day he would tell me, "Something's going on at work. I don't have a good feeling about my job." And each day, I would play Mary Poppins and tell him I was sure everything was fine. Imagine my surprise (much less his and the other employees' surprise) when he called me on December 3 to tell me he no longer had a job. It was surreal.

I encouraged my husband when I really had no idea what tomorrow would bring for us and our autistic son. But I remember very distinctly that I was not worried. That, in and of itself, was the Lord's work.

What followed was a great adventure. A letter my husband wrote to a newspaper brought us much media attention, including many interviews for both print and television. We awoke one Sunday morning to a phone call from a man in Wisconsin from a fellow father of a child with autism. He asked if my husband was, "the Mark Lindquist who's on the cover of the New York Times with his son." We, of course, knew of the interview, but thought the story would be tucked away inside the paper. Needless to say, we rushed to the nearest Starbucks to buy several copies.

What ensued was a scene right out of *It's a Wonderful Life*. We received countless phone calls from all over the country, mainly from fathers of children with disabilities. One such man even paid our COBRA payments for three months! Many sent letters of encouragement and money to help pay for our son's therapies. It was thrilling to see how many people cared about us and had loving, generous hearts.

Of course, there were times of deep sadness for my husband, and there were times of tremendous heartache for others affected by Enron's demise. We were not oblivious to the pain of so many, and we prayed for them as well as prayed for a job for Mark.

It was just before Christmas, so we knew it would be a slim one materially. However, we were blessed by so many, including the Salvation Army which was present at a job fair for all the former Enron employees. Although we told them we didn't need help nearly as much as some, they insisted that we go ahead and sign up with them. I remember crying when they insisted we do so, and crying again when we received gift cards to buy gifts for our children.

Of all these things, the most amazing miracle of all involved our faith. After all, a job is security. It is such a part of us that we tend to feel a false sense of control of our lives, our finances, and our decisions. When that job is stripped away, we either despair or turn back to the sufficiency of Christ.

We had the most wonderful Christmas! We did everything that was "free" to do in and around the Houston area. We drove around looking at Christmas lights several times a week, went to festivals, spent more time together as a family, and spent less money on the holiday than ever before. What should have been devastation was a revelation! Focusing more on the things not of this world made our time precious and meaningful. Our Christmases have been like this ever since then.

The most exciting part was that we were given an opportunity to share God's loving faithfulness with so many others. Every interview was another chance to tell the world that we were blessed even without a job and knew that God would take care of us! How I hope to this day that it touched someone!

(Incidentally, my husband got a job with Enron Credit Union and then lost that job also when countless customers closed their accounts – it was like a follow-up course in trusting God!)

Are you living out a revelation or devastation? Are you leaning on the promise of Christ that He will never leave nor forsake you? Does the enemy have you pinned down on the mat or are you wearing the whole armor of God as you live in this fallen world?

In Thought

"Dear Lord, thank You for being my sufficiency, my friend, my constant companion. Thank You that Your ways are higher than my ways. Please remind me of Your promises and help me not to worry. I want to shine for You. Please help me not to block the miracles You have for me. Amen."

In Word

- *Therefore I tell you, do not worry about your life, what you will eat or drink; or about your body, what you will wear. Is not life more than food, and the body more than clothes? Look at the birds of the air; they do not sow or reap or store away in barns, and yet your heavenly Father feeds them. Are you not much more valuable than they?* Matthew 6:25-26 NIV

- *Do not store up for yourselves treasures on earth, where moths and vermin destroy, and where thieves break in and steal. But store up for yourselves treasures in heaven.* Matthew 6:19-21 NIV

In Deed

Write about a time in your life when you felt devastated, but the Lord turned your mourning into dancing. Go back and read it on a regular basis to remind you of God's faithfulness.

Kim Lindquist

239

Week 10 Notes

_____

_____

_____

_____

_____

_____

_____

_____

_____

_____

_____

_____

_____

_____

_____

_____

_____

71
Free Bandicoot

My child, pay attention to what I say.
Listen carefully to my words.
Proverbs 4:20 NLT

One of my college roommates, Jen, was an animal lover – a trait I'll admit that I do not share. So although she really wanted a sweet little dog to scurry around our apartment, what we compromised on was a hamster. She searched far and wide for the perfect pet and finally settled on a Russian Dwarf Hamster she named Bandicoot.

Since we were in college during the beginning of the Internet era when websites were new and exciting, one of our assignments was to design a basic website that gave information about ourselves. On Jen's website, she wrote about her love of animals and mentioned her new pet, Bandicoot. She posted her site to the web and thought nothing more of it…until she started receiving strange emails from random people she didn't know with demands that she "free Bandicoot" immediately.

She went back to her website and finally understood what went wrong. What she *meant* to write was something along the lines of, "I love animals, but my roommate doesn't. So the only pet she'll let me have is a Russian Dwarf Hamster that I keep in a cage in my bedroom." The problem was that she accidentally omitted one key word: *hamster*. Suddenly the demands that she free Bandicoot made perfect sense.

She issued a correction on her website and even our professors had quite a good laugh at the innocent mistake, but as English majors, we learned an important lesson that day. Sometimes it's enough to get the main idea of a message and let the details disappear in the background. But other times…Every. Single. Word. Is. Important.

Strangely enough, I often think about Bandicoot when I read the Bible. There are times when I read quickly and lazily, flying over the words like a crop duster. I skim the surface just enough to get the main idea, but don't settle on anything long enough to feel the weight of each individual word. Not surprisingly, I don't get much out of those times of reading. But other times, when I slow down and prayerfully consider every word and detail as I'm reading, God's Word seems to jump off the page and settle into my heart.

What about you? How carefully are you reading your Bible? When you consider that the Bible is a love letter written straight from God's heart to yours, doesn't that make you want to slow down and savor every word? It's the difference between *reading* the Scriptures and *meditating* on them. To meditate on something simply means to ponder it, to reflect upon it, or to mull it over in your mind. "My eyes stay open through the watches of the night, that I may meditate on your promises" (Psalm 119:148 NIV). And when it comes to the Bible, it's not enough to simply read the main idea and let the details disappear in the background. Instead, we should read carefully and intentionally, meditating on God's message in such a way that not a single word falls away. Because when He speaks – Every. Single. Word. Is. Important.

In Thought

"Dear Lord, thank You for the Bible. Thank You that its message is so timeless and so relevant that it can speak to me in any and all circumstances. Help me not take Your words for granted. I pray that Your Spirit would speak to my heart as I read and that I would learn to meditate on Your words daily. Amen."

In Word

- *When your words came, I ate them; they were my joy and my heart's delight, for I bear your name, O LORD God Almighty.* Jeremiah 15:16 NIV
- *Every word of God is flawless; he is a shield to those who take refuge in him. Do not add to his words, or he will rebuke you and prove you a liar.* Proverbs 30:5-6 NIV
- *All Scripture is inspired by God and is useful to teach us what is true and to make us realize what is wrong in our lives. It corrects us when we are wrong and teaches us to do what is right. God uses it to prepare and equip his people to do every good work.* 2 Timothy 3:16-17 NLT
- *My child, pay attention to what I say. Listen carefully to my words. Don't lose sight of them. Let them penetrate deep into your heart, for they bring life to those who find them, and healing to their whole body.* Proverbs 4:20-22 NLT
- *I tell you the truth, until heaven and earth disappear, not the smallest letter, not the least stroke of a pen, will by any means disappear from the Law until everything is accomplished.* Matthew 5:18 NIV

In Deed

- Read Psalm 119 every day for a week.
- List several synonyms for Scripture, for example, *precepts, word, law.*
- List several benefits of Scripture, for example, triumph over sin (v. 11); strength (v. 28); direction (v. 105).

Emily Ryan

72
Marching Onward in Faith

A final word: Be strong in the Lord and in his mighty power. Put on all of God's armor so that you will be able to stand firm against all strategies of the devil. For we are not fighting against flesh-and-blood enemies, but against evil rulers and authorities of the unseen world, against mighty powers in this dark world, and against evil spirits in the heavenly places.
Ephesians 6:10-12 NLT

When I was young my family attended mass occasionally but never Sunday school. But about the time I was five, my father decided that would change, and we would join an Episcopalian church. I think he viewed that as somewhat middle ground between my mother's Catholic faith and his Baptist upbringing.

Wearing a new dress with a starched, white pinafore, I made my first acquaintance with Sunday school and I loved it! At story time, I sat rapt as the teacher read stories that were totally new to me and almost unbelievable. Later I worked diligently on my coloring page since, even at five, I believed that staying in the lines was a rule that must be obeyed. But snack time with red punch and cookies was probably my favorite. Though I don't indulge often, that combination still evokes the sweetest memories.

But what made the biggest impression on me was what happened at the end of class. All the boys and girls, about 25 of us, lined up and marched around the room singing "Onward Christian Soldiers." I clutched my coloring sheet tightly in one hand and my remaining cookie in the other and stomped my little Mary Jane's as hard as I could on the wooden floor. I didn't know the words at first, but by the last stanza I was singing, too: "Onward Christian soldiers marching as to war, with the cross of Jesus going on before." It took another 22 years before I actually enlisted in God's army, but He was ever faithful, and there were many times He reminded me of that day.

Since then, I've fought many battles and even been severely injured in a few, but I continued to march forth even when I wanted to retreat. I held on to the truth that, as Christians, we are to participate actively in the battles that come our way. They may be just a skirmish such as dealing with a difficult coworker, or they may be an all-out war with the diagnosis of a terminal illness. Whatever we face, we are called, as the song says, to give "Glory, laud and honor unto Christ the King." God in His perfect provision has equipped us with everything we need to fulfill that calling.

In Thought

"Father, sometimes the battles of this world seem so fierce I just want to give up. But I want to remember that You have given me the weapons I need. In Your strength I can withstand any onslaught of the enemy. Help me reflect Your mercy and grace to others during those times of struggle. Amen."

In Word

- *Be strong and courageous! Don't be afraid or discouraged because of the king of Assyria or his mighty army, for there is a*

246

power far greater on our side! He may have a great army, but they are merely men. We have the Lord our God to help us and to fight our battles for us! 2 Chronicles 32:7-8 NLT

- *Endure suffering along with me, as a good soldier of Christ Jesus. Soldiers don't get tied up in the affairs of civilian life, for then they cannot please the officer who enlisted them.* 2 Timothy 2:3-4 NLT

In Deed

When you wake up, read about the armor of God in Ephesians 6:13-17. Then pray through each piece of armor as you get dressed for the day.

Janie Southard

247

73
Andy's Name

---

*But rather rejoice, because your
names are written in heaven.*
Luke 10:20b KJV

My three-year-old son, James, loves to watch the *Toy Story* movies. After watching the second one for the umpteenth time, we decided it was time that he got his own *Toy Story* toy. After much debate and research of the product, we picked out a foot-long plastic space ranger named Buzz Lightyear. It had all the gizmos and functions that the character had on the movie, including a red light and sound effects for the laser, blue and green buttons on his chest causing Buzz to speak many different phrases and even another button that makes his wings pop out! To our delight, when James received his gift, he loved it! We would see him running through the house flying Buzz while saying his famous quote, "To infinity and beyond!"

After a few days, though, James came up to me and pushed Buzz into my lap. He pointed at his foot and said, "Mommy, where's Andy?" I turned the action figure over and saw nothing on his foot and I did not understand what James was asking.

"What do you mean?" I said. "Andy's not written on his foot."

Undeterred by my response, he again pointed to Buzz's foot and said, "Mommy, where's Andy?" It was then that I realized what he was asking me. In the movie, the little boy named Andy would write his name on the bottom of all his toys to show the world that they belonged to him. I grabbed a black marker and with James' help, we wrote the letters J-A-M-E-S on the bottom of his Buzz's foot. James carefully studied his name written there and then gave Buzz the biggest hug ever. "I love you, Buzz," he said. "You *are* mine!"

Watching my son that day showed me how very important it was that everyone knew that this toy belonged to him. When we receive Christ as our personal Savior, we are His! He writes our names in the Lamb's Book of Life and we belong to Him. No one else can have us, and it is as if God is saying to us, "I love you, My child. You *are* Mine!"

In Thought
"Lord, thank You for the miracle of salvation that You have given to me as a free gift. I immediately entered Your family as Your child, snatched from the grasp of death to life never to be lost to You. Lord, thank You for the assurance of Your great love. Amen."

In Word
- *Yet to all who did receive him, to those who believed in his name, he gave the right to become children of God.* John 1:12 NIV
- *For I am convinced that neither death nor life, neither angels nor demons, neither the present nor the future, nor any powers,*

neither height nor depth, nor anything else in all creation, will be able to separate us from the love of God that is in Christ Jesus our Lord. Romans 8:38-39 NIV

• *The Spirit himself testifies with our spirit that we are God's children.* Romans 8:16 NIV

In Deed

Remind yourself daily that the moment you accept Jesus' gift of salvation you instantly become His child and a much loved member of His family. Never forget that your name is written forever in the Lamb's Book of Life and nothing can separate you from the love of our heavenly Father.

Mikelle Challenger

74

The Runaway Ferris Wheel

For God has not given us a spirit of fear, but of power and of love and of a sound mind.
2 Timothy 1:7 NKJV

We always had such great family vacations when I was growing up. Many times, only Mom and I were traveling to the uttermost parts of Texas to see sand dunes, canyons, the Big Thicket, the world's largest jack rabbit (compliments of Odessa), and so many more unforgettable things.

But there was one trip that stands out in my mind. This time, my much older brother and my grandmother joined us. We were camping out (in a tent, of course, like "real" campers) and planned to go to Six Flags Over Texas in Arlington the next day.

As we all lay down in the pitch darkness to go to sleep, my brother began to fill my head with visions – but not of sugar plums! He proceeded to tell me about "the time when the Ferris wheel at Six Flags came off its axle and went rolling down the freeway."

You can just imagine what I was picturing. And if it could happen with the Ferris wheel, it could happen with other rides also! My anticipation of the next day was now tainted – if it happened before, it could happen again. Of course, acting "big," I said, "It did not!" But he was pretty convincing. I don't remember how long I thought about this, but I know it was not a short while. I don't remember what Mom or Grandmother said – I only remember the picture of apprehension in my head.

It didn't help matters when my brother also warned me about scorpions coming into the tent (don't you just love big brothers?), and when we awoke the next morning, my Grandmother had been stung by one! Hmmm…my brother warned about scorpions and one had come, so the Ferris wheel catastrophe could happen again!

Of course, we went to the amusement park the next day, and all the equipment functioned. However, I didn't bother to try the Ferris wheel. All went well, and think of all that time I spent afraid of something that wasn't even true!

Fear is interesting that way. It can be founded or unfounded. Rational or irrational. About things real or imagined. It is no respecter of persons, age, gender, belief system or intelligence level. It affects everyone. Fear is a powerful emotion and a powerful motivator.

Just think of all the things advertised in the world that play on our fear. That's not to say that some of these things are not wise to have. Homeowners insurance, flood insurance, auto insurance – these are things that can save you much money and stress if needed. But fear of loss is the motivator to buy it.

Is the course of our lives really going to be altered if we don't have those designer handbags, that particular car, that house beyond our means...all because we fear we won't look successful in this world? More seriously, is God not going to take care of us in spite of ourselves? He promises that He will never leave nor forsake us (Deuteronomy 31:6).

Christians are called to a life beyond fear. We don't have time to waste on fear when the world in dying without a Savior. We are to have a "spirit of boldness, not a spirit of timidity" in walking with the Spirit. Too often, we are afraid of what tomorrow will bring. What if I lose my job? What if I can't get a job? What if I never get married? What if my spouse never changes? What if I fail my class?

So much time is spent in worrisome fear instead of in fervent prayer. And like that fictional Ferris wheel story, our fear can run away at incredible speeds, hitting our dreams, our plans, our convictions and our testimony.

That's not to say that being a Christian means never being afraid. That emotion can crop up at any time. But we must remember that it is only an emotion; it does not control us. We are to have the mind of Christ (1 Corinthians 2:16) and walk according to the Holy Spirit (Romans 8:1). We may be called by God to do some things even though we feel afraid. He is faithful to keep us and to give us peace – our obedience cannot be based on feelings. We must pray "that utterance may be given to me, that I may open my mouth boldly to make known the mystery of the gospel" (Ephesians 6:19 NKJV).

In Thought

"Dear Lord, cast out fear from my mind today and replace it with Your peace that passes understanding. I pray for Your courage and boldness to be in me, that I may do all that You ask of me without hesitation. Thank You that the enemy cannot stand in the presence of Your power. Amen."

In Word

- *The LORD is with me; I will not be afraid. What can mere mortals do to me? The LORD is with me; he is my helper. I look in triumph on my enemies.* Psalm 118:6-7 NIV
- *Be strong and courageous. Do not be afraid or terrified because of them, for the LORD your God goes with you; he will never leave you nor forsake you.* Deuteronomy 31:6 NIV

In Deed

- Meditate on everything God has to say about peace in His Word.
- List any fears you are feeling, and then offer those up to God in prayer.
- Write Scriptures that specifically speak to the fears you have at this time, and refer to them on a regular basis.

Kim Lindquist

75

The Two-Headed Monster

The LORD himself goes before you and will be with you; he will never leave you nor forsake you. Do not be afraid; do not be discouraged.
Deuteronomy 31:8 NIV

I can remember one summer, when I was a teenager, sitting in the back seat of my parent's car. I was catching bits and pieces of their conversation that did not even concern me in the least, until I heard the words, "two-headed monster"! This definitely piqued my interest. I sat up and looked through the windshield to see a pickup truck waiting at the light ahead of us. Through their rear window I saw an outlined head and shoulders of a male sitting in the driver's seat. Snuggled up next to him was an outlined head and shoulders of a female passenger with the rest of the truck's cab very empty.

The traffic light seemed to stay red forever. My parents snickered while I studied the "two-headed monster." I could tell that the driver's arm was around the back of the seat and the girl had her head on his shoulder. I was imagining romantic, country music playing on the radio. The light turned green and the truck sped off.

"That reminds me of the preacher's story," Dad said.

"What preacher's story?" I asked.

This is what he told me: "An old couple who had been married for over 50 years had pulled up behind the car of a young, dating couple. They were sitting so close that it looked like the driver had two heads! The wife said to her husband, 'Remember when we used to sit like that?' And after no response, she turned to look at him and asked, 'Whatever happened to us? Why aren't we in love like that anymore?' With that, the husband looked at her for a moment and then calmly responded, 'Well, *I* am not the one that moved!'"

This anecdote is the picture of many Christians' relationship with Jesus. When we first come to the saving knowledge of Jesus Christ, we just cannot get enough of Him. We feel very close to Him. For a while, we pray and seek Him daily for everything. But as time goes by, we seem to draw further and further from Him. We become more and more independent and do most things in our own strength. Eventually, we find ourselves in a situation that forces us to turn back to our first love, Jesus. We pray desperately for Him to be with us and help us because we feel so alone when all the while, He never has moved away from us. He will never leave us or forsake us. He is exactly where He said He would be…waiting for us to call upon Him, waiting for us to seek Him daily and to have an abundant life with Him. It was never His intention just to "share a cab with us" on our way to heaven! When we cry out to God and say, "Why aren't we as close as we once were?" God is there, like that husband, saying, "My child, I am where I've always been…welcome back!"

In Thought

"Lord, thank you for the blessed assurance that once You come into my life as my Savior, You never leave. I claim that promise from Romans 8:38-39 this very moment. Please forgive me for my sins and for turning my back on You. I call on You, Lord, right now to restore my relationship with You and help me to walk daily with You. Amen."

In Word

And I am convinced that nothing can ever separate us from God's love. Neither death nor life, neither angels nor demons, neither our fears for today nor our worries about tomorrow—not even the powers of hell can separate us from God's love. No power in the sky above or in the earth below—indeed, nothing in all creation will ever be able to separate us from the love of God that is revealed in Christ Jesus our Lord. Romans 8:38-39 NLT

In Deed

Remember your conversion experience. Remember that moment you first prayed and asked Christ into your life to stay. Remember those days, weeks and months that followed and what your relationship was with Him. Now think about your present-day relationship with Jesus. How has it changed? Are you where you want to be in your relationship with your Savior? Are you where He wants you to be? If not, pray right now for forgiveness and that your relationship with Jesus is restored to walk daily with God.

Mikelle Challenger

76

God's Glory
in the Storm

*Yet what we suffer now is nothing compared
to the glory He will reveal to us later.*
Romans 8:18 NLT

From the safety of my living room I kept a watchful eye as the weather changed. The sky darkened with billowing clouds as the wind steadily blew the dampness in off the Gulf of Mexico. In the top branches of the tree that shades my patio, the highest, spindly ones that were swaying dramatically in the impending storm, sat a small bird. Her bright orange breast was puffed boldly out facing directly into the force of the wind.

Despite the onslaught, her black wings were not twitching in preparation for a flight to safety. Instead she had braced herself and was riding the branch up and down like a roller coaster. I was intrigued because this brave little bird appeared to welcome the possible dangers of the storm. It was as if she was saying, "I'm ready, bring it on!" She appeared to have no fear at all. She was ready for the thrill of a wild ride.

How often do we prepare for flight long before the crisis even arrives? Fear and worry are usually our first responses to whatever difficulties we might face, and our minds reel with the "What ifs?" and the "I can'ts." We would rather relax in ease and comfort than go through life-altering hardship. Yet it is in the most trying situations where God often reveals Himself the most.

Long ago, when faced with truly catastrophic events, Job pleaded with God for an explanation for his suffering. His friends were quick to say that he was merely reaping the consequences of his sin and should immediately repent. But God challenged Job to remember that it was He, the Almighty, who was in control of every circumstance that touched Job's life. After losing his family, his wealth and even his health, Job experienced God's overwhelming love and restoration. He was able to tell God, "I had only heard about you before, but now I have seen you with my own eyes" (Job 42:5 NLT).

If you're not currently experiencing a difficult time in your life, you may soon. The fact is that all of us will go through periods of testing, pruning and growth. As Jesus promised, "In this world you will have trouble. But take heart! I have overcome the world" (John 16:33 NIV). So while none of us enjoy obstacles or difficult times, we should use those times to open our eyes even wider to the glory and power of Christ.

In Thought

"Dear God, when trials come, I want my first response to be trust in You. Help me to see that the storms in my life have been uniquely designed by You so that I will know You better and experience Your infinite love and mercy. Amen."

In Word

- *Then the Lord answered Job from the whirlwind: "Who is this that questions my wisdom with such ignorant words? Brace yourself like a man, because I have some questions for you, and you must answer them.* Job 38:1-3 NLT
- *So the Lord blessed Job in the second half of his life even more than in the beginning.* Job 42:12a NLT

In Deed

Use a concordance to dig deeper into God's Word for Scriptures regarding your current circumstances. Check with someone in your local Christian bookstore or church library if you need additional help or resources as well.

Janie Southard

77

The Princess Bride

I will greatly rejoice in the LORD, my soul shall be joyful in my God; for He has clothed me with the garments of salvation, He has covered me with the robe of righteousness, as a bridegroom decks himself with ornaments, and as a bride adorns herself with her jewels.
Isaiah 61:10 NKJV

I remember every detail of planning my wedding. The multicolored bridesmaid dresses that could easily be worn to more than just the wedding, the cakes – one with a castle and Cinderella's pumpkin-turned-coach, the tons of multicolored balloons that floated all over the room of my reception, and on and on.

Of course, there was a bit of vengeance involved in the planning. Being the last of many of my girlfriends from high school to get married, I had been in quite a few weddings! My bridesmaid dresses that hung in the closet spanned the entire 80's decade. It was time for some payback, so I had 22 attendants in my wedding! It was amazing, and somewhat like the makings of a Broadway musical.

The planning of the wedding was almost as exciting as the actual day – it was a foretaste of what was to come on that special day. But nothing was more important than the marriage that was about to start. The fact that I would be one in Christ with a man who also loved the Lord was beyond description. The little mishaps of the day were humorous to me; nothing would put a damper on this glorious occasion. Even when I saw the video and the photos later, I loved that everything was not "perfect."

The little bridesmaid was scowling, the nephew was crying because he thought he was losing his aunt, the little groomsman was fidgeting, etc. But nothing mattered above the fact that we were now husband and wife. What happened to our spirits far surpassed anything on the outside.

Imagine, then, what a glorious occasion it will be when Jesus returns to take His Bride, the Church, home with Him forever! We are His beloved, and He has prepared a place for us in eternity. But we are not waiting to be married to Him; we are married to Him now. Our "wedding day" was the day we were saved by grace through Jesus Christ and at that moment received the promise of eternal life.

Before our marriage to Christ, there were no flowers to order, no cakes to pick out, and no special clothes to wear for the occasion. We came to Him just as we were, in blue jeans or in our pajamas, and became His.

But, like our earthly marriages, what happened internally is the miracle of the union. It is this inward transformation that shows through to a watching world. We are to be concerned with heavenly things rather than earthly things…we are to be concerned with being respectful, loving, reverent spouses of Jesus Christ our King. It is out of our love for Him that we behave differently through the power of His Holy Spirit whom He gave to us.

A new bride with no desire to know her husband or spend time with him would seem absurd to most of us. So it is when we do not live out our salvation – when we are more concerned with the outside adornment of our bodies, our homes, our cars, or even our churches than we are with growing to know the Lord more and more with each passing day.

Are you living out your marriage to Christ with reverence and a sense of loyalty? Are you meditating on His Word and seeking His face to know Him better? Do you have an earnest desire to grow more like Christ?

In Thought

"Dear Lord, please place in me a fervent desire to know You more...to be more like You. Please help me to return to my first love, to the kind of love I had when I first was saved by Your grace. I ask that You keep my mind steadfastly on You and Your ways rather than the ways of this world."

In Word

* *Create in me a clean heart, O God, and renew a steadfast spirit within me. Do not cast me away from Your presence, and do not take Your Holy Spirit from me.* Psalm 51:10-11 NKJV
* *For you were once darkness, but now you are light in the Lord. Walk as children of light (for the fruit of the Spirit is in all goodness, righteousness, and truth), finding out what is acceptable to the Lord. And have no fellowship with the unfruitful works of darkness, but rather expose them.* Ephesians 5:8-11 NKJV

In Deed

Spend some time with the Lord today. After praying that He will reveal what He wants to tell you, spend time in His Word. Look up Scriptures that deal with the attributes of God such as loving, kind, compassionate, merciful and just. Make a list of these attributes on a piece of paper with the Scripture references next to them. You can also list the fruits of the Spirit we've been given. Review this list each day this week and pray to live more like our Lord.

Kim Lindquist

Week 11 Notes

_____

_____

_____

_____

_____

_____

_____

_____

_____

_____

_____

_____

_____

_____

_____

_____

78
Need a Lift?

---

*The Lord upholds all those who fall and
lifts up all who are bowed down.*
Psalm 145:14 NIV

I've always been independent, even as a child. I picked out my own clothes, fixed my own hair, and even went to church alone on the bus in the early years. The Sundays I spent in Children's Church were some of the most exciting, most interesting times I'd ever experienced. And though the church was huge to my six-year-old eyes and the hallways were a little scary at times, once I found my seat and the service began, it was always worth any hesitations I'd felt before.

One Sunday after the service ended, I was walking up a long flight of stairs towards my Bible study classroom. The stairs seemed steeper that day, the climb longer, and the red glow from the stain glass window, spookier. It took some work to maneuver the stairs while clutching my lime green Precious Moments Bible in my arms, so at the halfway landing, I paused to readjust. Just when I was stepping up to the second set of stairs, I felt a strong pair of arms lift me up from behind and carry me the rest of the way to the top. I had no idea where the hands came from; I just felt the benefit of their strength and knew that they were hands I could trust. The moment my feet were planted back on the floor, I whipped my head around to find my dad who apparently had been behind me the whole time watching me be "independent" from the shadows. "It looked like you needed a lift," he said. And I guess I did.

It's when the climb is the hardest that we need a lift from our Father the most. But sometimes, in this world that thrives on independence and pride, we never stop to readjust during our obstacles and challenges. If anything, it's when the times are the hardest that our independent, prideful natures kick in and we push ourselves that much more.

"The Lord upholds all those who fall and lifts up all who are bowed down" (Psalm 145:14 NIV). It's more difficult to lift someone up when he's moving than it is to lift him up when he's still. God wants to help us through our times of trouble, but most of the time we never give Him the chance. We're too busy moving, climbing, trying, working and doing it on our own to pause on the landing and readjust.

Are the stairs in front of you high? Is your climb steep? Pause for awhile. Pray. Be still long enough for God to have a chance to lift you up. He promises in His Word that He will.

In Thought

"Heavenly Father, help me be still for awhile and rest at the foot of the Cross. Quiet my mind so that I might hear You, and weigh down my feet that I might not keep walking away from You. Forgive me for not pausing often enough to readjust my eyes to You, and lift me up, Lord, for the climb ahead of me is steep. Amen."

In Word

- *He lifted me out of the slimy pit, out of the mud and mire; he set my feet on a rock and gave me a firm place to stand.* Psalm 40:2 NIV
- *For he will command his angels concerning you to guard you in all your ways; they will lift you up in their hands, so that you will not strike your foot against a stone.* Psalm 91:11-12 NIV
- *He has brought down rulers from their thrones but has lifted up the humble.* Luke 1:52 NIV
- *Humble yourselves before the Lord, and he will lift you up.* James 4:10 NIV
- *Humble yourselves, therefore, under God's mighty hand, that he may lift you up in due time.* 1 Peter 5:6 NIV

In Deed

For the next week or so, don't focus on *doing* anything. Instead, pause. Be still. Be quiet. Stop running so hard and give the Lord, your heavenly Father, a chance to lift you up.

Emily Ryan

79

Never, Ever Plant Mexican Petunias

But the Lord said to Samuel, "Do not consider his appearance or his height, for I have rejected him. The Lord does not look at the things man looks at. Man looks at the outward appearance, but the Lord looks at the heart."
1 Samuel 16:7 NIV

A few years ago a friend of my mother-in-law offered me a beautiful little plant with a delicate purple flower. She promised me it would quickly multiply and I would soon be gazing upon a garden blooming profusely with color. I jumped at the chance for a quick and inexpensive way to populate my new, mostly empty, garden.

While I waited to reap my bonanza of Mexican petunias, I planted some other things. Among them were several small antique rose bushes luscious with sweet fragrance and several types of lilies all surrounding a Texas Mountain Laurel tree at the center of the garden.

Little did I know that while my beautiful roses grew to unexpected proportions, lurking in the darkness of the rich soil were the roots of Mexican petunias. It wasn't long before the little lavender flowers became a nuisance. They were nipping at the feet of my roses and boldly pushing their way between the stones of the pathways and around the rocks that formed the garden's border.

Searching for a solution, I asked a fellow gardener if she was familiar with the plant and her instant reply was, "Oh yes! It's the plant from…" Let's just say my friend felt the origins of this particular plant were from a very warm place far below the soil. Unfortunately, she continued, eradication of it was almost impossible.

I was aghast! Through my horticultural ignorance I had allowed this demon plant into the haven of my lovely garden that I hoped would be an oasis of peace and beauty. Early the next morning I began to hack away at each little plant, pulling up as much of the root as possible. As He so often does when I'm in my garden, the Lord began to speak. "This is exactly what happens to your heart when you allow the enemy to sneak in," God said. "He entices you with promises of quick satisfaction or easy success. If you allow his lies to take root in the garden of your heart, they will spread like weeds and choke out My truth that is supposed to flourish there."

If I had only waited patiently, I would have seen how quickly the other plants grew in the warmth and humidity of our climate filling my garden with an array of color and delightful fragrance. But I had wanted immediate results. Now I was paying the price for my wrong choice. To rid the garden of this menace would involve backbreaking labor and incredible amounts of time as I meticulously removed each plant.

Many of us have succumbed to the same ploy of the enemy who tries to convince us that looking good on the outside is more important than cultivating spiritual beauty. We'll spend hours working out at the gym, but can't seem to find time to read or study the Bible. Costly facial creams and hair color might make our outward appearance more attractive, but they do nothing for the sin that lurks beneath the surface. It seems easier, and certainly quicker, to fix up what we see reflected in the mirror each morning. But if we allow God to apply the healing balm of His word to our hearts and minds, the effects are immediate and last for eternity.

In Thought

"Lord, I want to focus on what is important to You. Your Word tells me it is my spirit that You see, not my outward appearance. I want to make the choices that would create in me a beauty that reflects You to everyone I encounter. Never let me forget that it is not expensive creams but daily cleansing in my heart that will yield the unfading beauty that I seek. Amen."

In Word

Your beauty should not come from outward adornment such as braided hair and the wearing of gold jewelry and fine clothes. Instead it should be that of your inner self, the unfading beauty of a gentle and quiet spirit, which is of great worth in God's sight. 1 Peter 3:3-4 NIV

In Deed

- If you set a regular appointment to have your hair done, or go to the gym, make a daily appointment to read and study God's Word.
- Instead of chasing after the latest fads in clothing, choose to chase after God. Wanting to look neat and fit, even beautiful or handsome, is not wrong, but your goal should be to reflect the beauty of the Lord with a gentle and quiet spirit.

Janie Southard

80
Walkabout

Be still, and know that I am God.
Psalm 46:10a NIV

When I attended Azusa Pacific University, a private Christian university in northeast Los Angeles, California, I was chosen to be a Resident Advisor. I was told that at the beginning of the next school year I must participate in a ten-day, Walkabout experience in Yosemite National Park. I was concerned about this at first, but was told not to worry, so I did not. After spending a great summer relaxing back in Houston, I returned just a few hours before it was time to load onto the buses en route to Yosemite. I did not realize my mistake in scheduling my flight until it was too late, but I had missed all of the training meetings for the trip. I shrugged my shoulders and thought, "Walkabout must mean some kind of camping trip." I envisioned a camp site with cute little pup tents surrounding a little fish-stocked lake where we could canoe and fish with pre-baited hooks followed by s'mores every night around a campfire. That could not have been further from the truth!

A few days later, I found myself sitting on the side of a mountain wearing the warmest clothes I had brought with me. I had my Bible, three contraband Jolly Rancher candies, and a bottle of water. I was shocked to be told that I would spend the next forty-eight hours fasting and being in complete isolation in an assigned area. I was happy at first because, at least, I was not going to have to trudge up the side of the mountain again with the heaviest pack in the world on my back, like we had done the last three days. My poor feet were covered in First-Aid tape from blisters from my new hiking boots. But the relief I had felt took a sour turn when I had to walk in circles all night due to the extreme frigid conditions. I will never forget the next morning standing at the edge of my area watching the sun's rays creep toward me and then jumping up and down for joy when the warmth covered my body! I spent that entire morning sleeping like a lizard on a rock, soaking up the sun. When I was brought more water and a sleeping bag for the second night, I was beside myself with gratitude!

I could go on and on about the hardness of the time of isolation or the physical strain of going up and down the mountains. But, mixed in with the difficult memories are the sweet ones, like the encouragement I was given by those around me. I have yet to eat pancakes that tasted as good as that morning after coming out of the fast. But the memory that I hope will never fade is the quietness and the stillness that I experienced on that mountaintop. For the first time in my life, I was still. It was such sweet, uninterrupted hours reading God's Word, praying and listening for His voice. It changed my life and now, amid the stress of each day, I long for that quiet time again with Him. When we returned to campus, I finally asked a question I should have before I accepted the position, "Why ten days for Walkabout?" Their answer did not surprise me. "It's just enough time to break you!"

There are times in our lives when God places us where we have to be still before Him. Maybe it is during the death of a loved one, a loss of a job or a relocation where you find yourself all alone. In those times of isolation, we finally turn to our Savior and listen to His voice. Whether you are on a mountain top celebrating the sun's rays or trying to keep warm in the darkness, remember that the Lord is with you.

273

In Thought

"Lord, help me to take time today to be still and listen for Your voice. I want to rest in Your shadow because You are my refuge and strength. I want to know You daily. Show me Scriptures that speak to my heart. Remind me that I am never alone. I love You. Amen."

In Word

Whoever dwells in the shelter of the Most High, will rest in the shadow of the Almighty. I will say of the LORD, "He is my refuge and my fortress, my God, in whom I trust." Psalm 91:1-2 NIV

In Deed

- Take a day, an hour or even ten minutes to be still before the Lord.
- Find a passage of Scripture from God's Word to read and to meditate on today.

Mikelle Challenger

81

Pleasing Everybody

While he was still speaking, a bright cloud enveloped them, and a voice from the cloud said, "This is my Son, whom I love; with him I am well pleased. Listen to him!"
Matthew 17:5 NIV

Looking through the cabinets and fridge trying to find something to cook for dinner is often a challenge. But one night, for some reason, it was even harder than most. One member of the family was trying to diet, one was super active playing sports at school, and therefore, could eat the side of a house, and my daughter was toying with the idea of becoming a vegetarian. Anyone could see my dilemma. I could make Frito pie, a cold-weather favorite, but it's not low calorie, and definitely not vegan. Grilled chicken would have been great for three of the four of us, but I forgot to thaw the chicken out. I could take the easy road and make it an all vegetable (from cans) meal, but the football player would act like he was starving to death, and quite frankly, so would I.

And to add to the uncertainty, I still needed to return those emails, proofread my husband's proposal for his meeting the next day, and send out the invitations for the book club's social. Speaking of book club, they would be here the next day, and I still needed to clean the bathroom and vacuum the den (and finish that book!).

As parents, we tend to focus on pleasing our children. As husbands and wives, we want to please our spouses. As employees, we want to please our bosses. We are always trying to please someone. But as Christians, our focus should be on pleasing our Father. We should want His approval above all others. God delights in His children. He desires for our focus to be on Him. Jesus remains our pattern for our lives. His life was declared "pleasing" in the sight of God by the Father Himself (Matthew 17:5). We must seek to please not man but God. He created us for His pleasure. God takes delight in us, not just in what we do.

Our children will not starve if they don't like what we're having for dinner one night. Our spouses should not depend on us for being pleased and content. Our friends will never be satisfied by us. Focus on God and His pleasure and all of the other things will take their place in this life.

In Thought

"O Father, I want to please You. Let me stop and focus on making You happy with my actions, my words and my thoughts. I want You to be first priority in my life. Help me to be more aware of Your presence. Amen."

In Word

- *For God is working in you, giving you the desire and the power to do what pleases Him.* Philippians 2:13 NLT
- *May the God of peace, who through the blood of the eternal covenant brought back from the dead our Lord Jesus, that great Shepherd of the sheep, equip you with everything good for doing his will, and may he work in us what is pleasing to him, through Jesus Christ, to whom be glory for ever and ever. Amen.* Hebrews 13:20-21 NIV

In Deed

As you find yourself trying to please everyone and becoming frazzled, stop and ask God, "How can I please You?"

BJ Massa

82
Untying the Ribbon

For the mind set on the flesh is death, but the mind set on the Spirit is life and peace.
Romans 8:6 NASB

I saw a message the other day written in a most unusual place—the side of a woman's handbag—that read, "Life is a gift, untie the ribbon." I started thinking. Am I truly living the life Christ died for me to have? Or do I still exist in the lifestyle I knew when I first met Him and accepted the gift of salvation? I had to check old attitudes, behaviors and past relationships.

When I did, I realized that I had shed many of my past preconceived, worldly notions in favor of the Word of God. For example, I used to be very pro-choice. I believed that if a woman felt she needed an abortion, she should be able to get one legally and without risks to her health. I had had this attitude since girlhood when a friend of mine became pregnant after being drugged at a party. I was angry that she had to go to an unsanitary, unsafe place to get rid of a child she'd had no say in conceiving. After the abortion, she was sterile. It seemed so unfair to me. I actually cheered when Roe vs. Wade was passed. I wasn't a Christian then. Later, after coming to know Christ and understanding the sovereignty of God, I realized that we preempt God's authority when we decide who should live and who should die. And none of us has the right to presume we know better than God!

Many people have accepted the marvelous gift of salvation in Christ but have yet to untie the ribbon around that gift. Many are still living worldly lives unaware of the miraculous transformation awaiting them when they untie the ribbon on this most precious gift. When we surrender our lives to Christ, we become, the Bible says, new creations! The untying of the ribbon is a surrender of our old lives, attitudes, choices, and sometimes, relationships. But what we gain from God is so much sweeter than anything the world has to offer. First, we are returned to spiritual oneness with the Father in heaven through the deposit of the Holy Spirit which seals us against the day of redemption. Second, the indwelling Spirit begins a transforming process in our lives. Justified by faith in Christ's death and resurrection, the Spirit guides us in the sanctification process as we become more and more like our Savior. We gain the mind of Christ which is spiritual, stable and secure – if we allow the Spirit to do His mighty work. We untie the ribbon by surrendering ourselves to the Spirit of God.

Are you surrendered to the Spirit today? Surrendering to Christ is not an option for Christians, especially if we want to have the abundant life He promises us in the Bible. A surrendered life is a life of servanthood to our Savior and Master, Jesus Christ. Untie the ribbon on your gift today; you'll never regret having done so, for you will reap a reward in peace, love and joy which surpasses all understanding.

In Thought

"Father in heaven, I come before You with praise and worship for the awesome plan of salvation that has set me free from the law of sin and death. I believe that Christ lived, died and rose on the third day as the Bible says in payment for my sin. Now, I seek to be like my Savior, Jesus Christ. Help me, oh God, to untie the ribbon on my gift of salvation. Make me like my Savior through the transforming power of Your Holy Spirit which dwells in me. Help me to bring my mind, attitudes, choices and relationships in line with Your holy Word. Amen."

In Word

* *And so, dear brothers and sisters, I plead with you to give your bodies to God because of all he has done for you. Let them be a living and holy sacrifice—the kind he will find acceptable. This is truly the way to worship him. Don't copy the behavior and customs of this world, but let God transform you into a new person by changing the way you think. Then you will learn to know God's will for you, which is good and pleasing and perfect.* Romans 12:1-2 NLT

* *So all of us who have had that veil removed can see and reflect the glory of the Lord. And the Lord—who is the Spirit—makes us more and more like him as we are changed into his glorious image.* 2 Corinthians 3:18 NLT

In Deed

* Do an attitude check. Do your attitudes reflect those of God? If not, pray for discernment and strength to change them. Old attitudes are like diapers and need to be changed frequently.

* Pray for direction daily, and untie your ribbon by surrendering every area of your life to His will.

* Finally, read your Bible daily. It renews our minds, hearts and relationship with God. It is our love letter from Him to us, and in it He gives us all we need to follow Him.

Patricia Dixon

83
Seeing God in an Ultrasound

Each of you should use whatever gift you have received to serve others, as faithful stewards of God's grace in its various forms. If anyone speaks, they should do so as one who speaks the very words of God. If anyone serves, they should do so with the strength God provides, so that in all things God may be praised through Jesus Christ. To Him be the glory and the power forever and ever. Amen.
1 Peter 4:10-11 NIV

I remember the first time I heard about a pregnancy center's need for an ultrasound technician. It was Sanctity of Life Day and I was sitting comfortably in my favorite spot in the worship center of our church in Boca Raton, Florida. While I had always wanted to serve the Lord with my registered nursing degree, I always thought I would do so by caring for the elderly. However, as I sat listening to the call for volunteers, my palms started to sweat and my heart began to beat wildly, and I realized that God was giving me a new desire to serve Him. It helped that my husband said, "Mikelle, I can see *you* doing those ultrasounds," but I still wanted more confirmation from the Lord. I wanted to know that volunteering as a sonographer was what I was *really* supposed to do. The affirmation did not come until sometime later, during one of my final teaching ultrasounds.

My client that day was a teenage girl who was accompanied by her very angry mother. Her story was complicated, as most of them are. The mother had an abortion when she was a teenager and it was a devastating experience for her. When she became pregnant again, at the age of 17, she fought pressure from her parents and had a baby girl. Now, less than twenty years later, that daughter was pregnant out of wedlock. I thought the mother would have been pro-life due to her past experience, but she was all the more insistent that an abortion was the solution.

The daughter was silent and pale as she listened to her mother's tirade about the ruined future she had ahead of her if she kept this baby. Hopelessness crept over me as I realized that not only was the counseling we had offered ineffective, but the ultrasound seemed to be having no effect on them either. I found myself at a loss for words, so I just started praying that God would intervene!

Suddenly, I realized the mother had stopped talking and the daughter was smiling for the first time. They were both looking at the ultrasound screen where the perfect profile of the baby appeared and its little hand started waving back and forth and back and forth. I had never seen a fetus do this before or since. It was truly a miracle because of the amazing effect it had on not only the daughter, but the mother as well! I never did hear what the final outcome was with that family, but I do know that all of us were crying as we entered the counseling room together. Their hardened hearts had been softened by a living miracle from God that day!

Today, I am still doing ultrasounds in a crisis pregnancy center. If I ever begin to doubt if God really called me to this ministry, I simply remember that teenage girl, over eleven hundred miles away, five years ago, and I thank God for the many wonderful opportunities He has given me to serve Him in this way!

I learned that day that counseling and ultrasound technology is nothing without being truly plugged into Jesus' power source. He is the One who truly changes the hearts of the scared, hurt and angry. It is encouraging to know that we are simply the instruments He uses to change the hearts of those around us. We just have to show up and be ready to be amazed at God's miraculous work! Listen carefully, and do not miss out on what God may be calling you to do for Him today!

In Thought

"Lord, I am nothing without You. Thank You for the opportunity to serve You and use the gifts You gave me to honor You. You are the vine and I am the branches, and apart from Your power source I can do nothing. Amen."

In Word

- *Remain in me, as I also remain in you. No branch can bear fruit by itself; it must remain in the vine. Neither can you bear fruit unless you remain in me. I am the vine; you are the branches. If you remain in me and I in you, you will bear much fruit; apart from me you can do nothing. If you do not remain in me, you are like a branch that is thrown away and withers; such branches are picked up, thrown into the fire and burned.* John 15:4-6 NIV
- *Yet you, LORD, are our Father. We are the clay, you are the potter; we are all the work of your hand.* Isaiah 64:8 NIV

In Deed

- If you are not currently serving the Lord with your gifts and talents, pray that the Lord impresses upon your heart exactly where He wants you to serve. Then, when you feel led to step up and serve, do not hesitate!
- If you are currently serving the Lord with your gifts and talents, pray that the Lord blesses you with confirmation that you are exactly where He wants you to be. As part of your service, take the time and effort to encourage and train those around you to serve as well.

Mikelle Challenger

84
The Trip Is Bountiful

Finally, brethren, whatever things are true, whatever things are noble, whatever things are just, whatever things are pure, whatever things are lovely, whatever things are of good report, if there is any virtue and if there is anything praiseworthy—meditate on these things.
Philippians 4:8 NKJV

In May 1985, I decided to take a trip with five friends – a road trip from Pasadena, Texas, to Canada. The six of us were all crammed into a van pulling a fishing boat, gear and luggage behind us! When I look back, it's downright amazing that six people in that small space all got along for that *long* trip up and back.

When we got to Tuscaloosa, Alabama, the van broke down. We weren't even halfway there, and the guys had to do a brake job in a parking lot! It was hot, we were already tired, and Canada seemed even further away. Needless to say, we prayed a lot and were back on the road later that day.

It was somewhat a sign of things to come!

In New York City, there was no place to park a van that size, so we had to walk from the outskirts of town to the heart of the city.

We spent our first night in Massachusetts, so we had to rotate drivers during the night, with the co-pilot keeping the driver awake (but the co-pilots often nodded off). When we got lost in Canada, I got out, thinking myself smart, and tried to use all the French I could remember from high school when we stopped at a gas station. I learned that my French was not at all their French!

The list of surprises continued. When we finally arrived at our camping spot, the boat sank and had to be retrieved from the freezing lake. I stayed in the van one day to stay warm while the others fished and a man with an M-16 on his shoulder walked right by the van – bear hunting! And, much to our dismay, we learned that we had traveled all that way at the wrong time of year to catch a lot of fish!

But if you were to ask me about that trip, I would tell you I had the time of my life! The mountains of Tennessee, the multicolored leaves near Boston, standing up through the sunroof as we drove through New York City as I waved to everyone and shouted "Hello," my first subway ride, Times Square, the gorgeous countryside of upper New York, Niagara Falls, seeing friends we'd not seen in years, meeting new ones who hosted us in their home in Wisconsin, the laughter, driving into Canada at sunrise and being amazed at how long the sunsets lasted! *These* are the things, and more, that made the biggest impressions on me.

In our journey with Christ, we face many obstacles. Sometimes on a daily basis, we are faced with situations and problems that can bring discouragement, frustration, doubt, grief and even impatience with our lot in life.

We know that we are more than conquerors in Jesus Christ and He is our overcomer. Not everything that is difficult is from Satan – it may be just a result of living in a fallen world. It goes all the way back to the Garden of Eden. Sometimes problems come as consequences of our or someone else's bad decisions. And, of course, there are those times when the Lord is allowing hardships to refine us like gold.

Regardless of why we are suffering, we sometimes find it impossible to "be content in everything," as Paul teaches in Philippians 4:11-13.

Our lives are not to be problem free. The Lord understands our grief during trials. He has suffered beyond what our minds can comprehend. At the same time, we are called to "give thanks in all circumstances; for this is God's will for you in Christ Jesus" (1 Thessalonians 5:18 NIV). We can live our lives recognizing all that the Lord does for and through us and see the beauty that He is and that He has made us as His children! Through the Holy Spirit, we see the Lord's spiritual protection of us, the everyday beauty of His creation, the miracles all around us, and the "little things" that happen to us on a regular basis that the world would call coincidence, but we know were God-ordained.

May the Lord give us His eyes to focus on the works of His hands in us and around us rather than our eyes that often stare at our difficulties and focus on this fallen world. We look forward to a future in His glory where there will be no more difficulties and no more tears!

In Thought

"Lord, thank You for making our lives adventurous. Even though we don't always understand why things are happening, please increase our faith in You. We want to have Your eyes, Your heart, Your mind. Please make us decrease and You increase. Amen."

In Word

- *I consider that our present sufferings are not worth comparing with the glory that will be revealed in us.* Romans 8:18 NIV
- *No, in all these things we are more than conquerors through Him who loved us.* Romans 8:37 NIV

In Deed

Look up in Scripture the many promises Jesus has made to us. Read and meditate on at least one promise each day for one month, and take note of how it encourages you. You may decide to keep reading His promises every day of the year!

Kim Lindquist

Week 12 Notes

85

The Pinkie Chronicles

Do everything without complaining or arguing.
Philippians 2:14 NIV

In the past six months, how much have you thought about your left pinkie finger? Has it been the first thing you've thought of when you woke up or the last thing on your mind as you drifted off to sleep? Probably not. In fact, it probably hasn't crossed your mind at all.

Although I don't give mine much thought anymore either, there was a time when I thought of little else. After breaking the 5th metacarpal bone in my left hand several years ago, my left pinkie finger was the source of much thought, many tears, countless prayers, and hundreds of dollars over about a six-month period.

I went through two surgeries, three physical therapists, and numerous hours of physical therapy trying to get my hand back to normal. When the healing process finally came to an end, I was grateful it was finally over, but also ashamed that I had not handled the pinkie episode very gracefully. If the truth be told, I realized how big a baby I had been about the whole thing. I griped about the inconvenience of going to therapy three times a week; I whined about the pain as if it were a terminal disease; and I remained depressed that I might never again be able to bend my pinkie more than thirty degrees.

Before the pinkie episode, I thought I was a pretty strong person. Now I know differently. I no longer contemplate how much I can handle, but rather realize how little it takes to break me. All it took was a silly little fracture and the partial impairment of only one tenth of my fingers for me to be reduced to a whiny crybaby.

Others have gone through so much more. And sadly, it took me almost six months to realize the only thing that makes my problems bigger than everyone else's is that...they're mine. However, I'm not alone.

If ever a group of people knew how to whine and complain, it was the Israelites. After God had done so much for them, I am amazed at how quickly they began to complain. In the passages surrounding Exodus 16, there is a reference to the Israelites' grumbling almost ten times! Keep in mind, this group of people had just witnessed one of the greatest miracles ever - the parting of the Red Sea. They had survived the ten plagues against the Egyptians and then marched across dry land to escape captivity; and the second they were free, they began to complain. They complained about the water, about the manna, about their leaders. They even whined because they weren't in captivity anymore.

And, as silly and ungrateful as the Israelites look to us today, frequently we're no better than they were. God answers our prayers day after day as He fulfills His promise to take care of us. Yet the minute something doesn't go exactly according to our plan, we grumble and complain. Perhaps we should all take a "non-alcoholic" approach to life from now on by cutting the "whine" from our lips. "Do everything without complaining or arguing, so that you may become blameless and pure, children of God without fault in a crooked and depraved generation, in which you shine like stars in the universe" (Philippians 2:14-15 NIV).

In Thought

"Dear Lord, please forgive my grumbling. You have blessed me more than I could ever deserve, yet I always seem to focus on the have-not's rather than the have's. Thank You for all that You give me, and thank You again for blessing me so generously. Amen."

In Word

- *I know what it is to be in need, and I know what it is to have plenty. I have learned the secret of being content in any and every situation, whether well fed or hungry, whether living in plenty or in want. I can do everything through him who gives me strength.* Philippians 4:12-13 NIV
- *Do everything without complaining or arguing, so that you may become blameless and pure, children of God without fault in a crooked and depraved generation, in which you shine like stars in the universe.* Philippians 2:14-15 NIV

In Deed

- Read Exodus 13-17 and notice how much God did for the Israelites. Did they spend more time thanking God or complaining?
- List your top five complaints. Now, turn them into something you can be thankful for.
- For example: Complaint: My left pinkie finger does not bend correctly. Blessing: Thank you, God, that I have both of my hands, all of my fingers, and generally great health. I am so thankful for that! --or-- Complaint: I don't make enough money. Blessing: Thank you, God, that I have a job when so many are unemployed. I am so grateful for that!

Emily Ryan

86
A Garden of Hope

---

*Let us hold fast the confession of our hope without
wavering, for He who promised is faithful.*
Hebrews 10:23 NKJV

I first learned what "esperanza" means when I was looking for a plant that would bear yellow blooms. Yellow flowers of any kind have always looked like happiness to me. As I saw these plants at a local nursery, I asked what they were. Knowing far too little Spanish, I had to ask the sales clerk what "esperanza" meant. "Hope," he said.

Hope. Having a child with a disability, I found I had been greatly lacking in feeling hope. Not that there wasn't any, of course. I just couldn't feel it.

I bought five plants that day and said, "I can always use more hope… I'll plant some!" Through the years, the plants have been through all kinds of phases. Some years they have done well, but in the winter of 2009, things looked pretty bleak. After everything had thawed out from the unusually hard Houston winter, my husband said, "We need to pull up those sticks on the side of the house."

I quickly defended my flower bed of hope and explained, "They're not dead. They just look dead. But if you scratch under the surface, you'll see that they are still green – that means they're alive."

When I later cut those "sticks" down to the ground, they came back the next year more beautiful than any of the years past. Now they are full, flourishing, healthy and beautiful. Pruning never looks pretty, but it is necessary for more growth.

That's how it is at times in our walk with Christ. He is our "ever-present help in trouble," (Psalm 46:1 NIV) even when we cannot see any hope with human intellect and reason. Things may look bleak, and we may even question Him at times…His timing, His methods, His answers. Nevertheless, our hope is in Christ because of what He endured on the cross to bring us an eternal hope.

He has given a "future hope for you, and your hope will not be cut off" (Proverbs 23:18 NIV). And may we remember that not only is hope not a mere feeling, but also that our "faith is the substance of things hoped for, the evidence of things not seen" (Hebrews 11:1 NKJV).

Plant some hope in someone's life today. Share the gospel in a loving manner so that he or she can share in the hope that you have.

In Thought

"Oh, Lord, how much I love You for making a way out of the darkness for me. I know that my very breath comes from You and You are the Lord of all. Grant to me a new understanding of Your love for me and of the hope I have in You in all situations of life – a hope that the lost do not have. Please put compassion in me for the lost, and help me to share You with them in a mighty way. Amen."

In Word

- *But sanctify the Lord God in your hearts: and be ready always to give an answer to every man that asketh you a reason of the hope that is in you with meekness and fear.* 1 Peter 3:15 KJV
- *Now faith is confidence in what we hope for and assurance about what we do not see.* Hebrews 11:1 NIV

In Deed

- Print out verses about hope and post these around your desk at work or around your home.
- Invite a lost friend over for coffee or dinner. Spend that time listening and pray that you would hear his or her heart. Then, pray for the words to share hope and the redeeming love of Christ.

Kim Lindquist

87

The Designer Purse

*For You formed my inward parts; You covered me in my
mother's womb. I will praise You, for I am fearfully and
wonderfully made; marvelous are Your works, and that
my soul knows very well.*
Psalm 139:13-14 NKJV

Sometime in the 1970's it became popular to carry a denim purse. It was the "in" thing at the time, and everyone had one!

My Grandmother McLaughlin, quite a seamstress, decided she would make one for me. It was a dark denim bag with a flap closure. It had silver brads on the flap and two front pockets with embroidered patches sewed on. I loved it! And, as is important to a young girl, I got compliments on it frequently.

One day, leaving one of my classes, I realized I didn't have my purse with me. Did I leave it in my locker, in P.E., in the previous class? My mind reeled with possibilities of where it could be, but I didn't find it anywhere. I left school that day heartbroken. The next day, I told the appropriate people in the office it was missing, but still to no avail.

Weeks passed and I knew I'd never see my prized possession again. I mentioned that it was missing to my good friend who was a year older than me and like a brother to me. Imagine my excitement when he found my purse in someone else's locker and returned it to me one day! He was my hero! I didn't care who had it, where he found it, or what was taken from it. All I cared about was having the purse again!

To this day, I cannot remember what was taken from me, only what was returned. And it wasn't just the purse that meant so much; it was the fact that it was a one-of-a-kind creation that my grandmother made for me! The value of my purse was in its *maker* and *designer*. It was a McLaughlin original!

We too are originals just like that purse! But who are we, mere humans, that we should have value in and of ourselves? With billions and billions of people in the world, who are we that God is mindful of us? (See Psalm 8.) We know God does not show favoritism, so why should He notice any of us?

Our value is not in ourselves but in our Maker! Our worth does not come from our talents, our personalities, our morality, our intelligence, our works, our jobs, our fame, our parental abilities or our children. Before Christ we were lost – confined to a "locker" of sin and shame. Our glorious paradise was stolen away by death and sin, and we needed a "hero" to rescue us.

By the loving sacrifice of Jesus Christ on a cruel instrument of death – the cross – we were rescued, redeemed and returned to our original owner! Praise be to our Father and to our Redeemer who makes us a "Designer People" of great value and worth!

In Thought

"Oh Lord, thank You that I am important to You. Thank You that I don't have to look for a reason to have self-esteem, but that I have Christ-esteem! Help me to reflect my worth in You through godly thinking, attitudes, words and deeds. Amen."

In Word

- *But you are a chosen generation, a royal priesthood, a holy nation, His own special people, that you may proclaim the praises of Him who called you out of darkness into His marvelous light; who once were not a people but are now the people of God, who had not obtained mercy but now have obtained mercy.* 1 Peter 2:9-10 NKJV
- *When I consider Your heavens, the work of Your fingers, the moon and the stars, which You have ordained, what is man that You are mindful of him, and the son of man that You visit him? For You have made him a little lower than the angels, and You have crowned him with glory and honor.* Psalm 8:3-5 NKJV

In Deed

The originality of creation reflects God's creativity, so find a place to be alone and spend time praising Him for making you so unique. Thank Him for your assets and your quirks alike.

Kim Lindquist

88
Road Trips and Righteousness

For we are strangers before you and sojourners, as all our fathers were. Our days on the earth are like a shadow and there is no abiding.
1 Chronicles 29:15 ESV

The roots of my family tree descend so deep into the red dirt of Alabama and South Carolina that hurricane force winds couldn't pry them loose. But despite my parents' best efforts to stay near kinfolk, Uncle Sam had other plans. When my father retired from the Air Force, we became part of a huge influx of new residents to the coastal prairie near Houston.

Astronauts were our neighbors and I babysat for their children. Reporters and news cameras were common sights in our neighborhood. But for my mother, all the hoopla about exploring space was overshadowed by the fact that her parents, brothers, aunts, uncles and cousins were at least 500 miles away.

However, my mama was an independent soul, and she would not allow mere miles to separate her from those she loved. If Daddy couldn't take time from work, she simply set off on her own with my brother and me nestled in the spacious back seat of our blue-finned Cadillac. In those days, it took two days to make a trip that today I make in about nine hours with the benefit of Interstate 10. But in the early sixties, it was slow going through little towns and large cities.

By the time we reached Gulfport, Mississippi, we were ready for fresh seafood. I didn't need my stomach to tell me it was time to eat. As soon as the stately antebellum mansions along the coast appeared my appetite immediately awakened. I stared intently out the window at their beauty wishing I could live in such storybook splendor.

The completion of Interstate 10 made the trip much faster and rest areas became familiar because we often picnicked. Not far from Houston was a rest stop my parents usually stopped for coffee and donuts when they felt the big city was safely behind us. Etched in my memory is the time we encountered what my brother and I called a "hobo." We shared our donuts with him as I glanced from his dirty face to the woods behind us that he called home.

When the time came to choose a college, it seemed natural that I pick LSU in Baton Rouge conveniently located just an exit off our normal route. Within a few years, it was I who began the I-10 pilgrimages with my own children taking them to see their grandparents who had retired to their home town in Alabama. All too soon the trips were prompted by funerals as my parents, aunts and uncles passed away.

It seems silly to me that memories of travel on an interstate highway could cause such emotion to well up within me. But it is literally a concrete reminder that I inherited more than just a love of road trips from my parents. From my flighty, hippy days of college to the trying times with a young family, my parents were a constant source of support as well as the source of generous amounts of grace and forgiveness. And just as the road we have so frequently traveled over the last 50 years has undergone much construction, so have I.

When I allowed God to intervene in my life, the road I traveled did not become easier, but there were a lot more satisfying rest stops along the way. As I immersed myself in His Word, my perspective on the trials I faced changed and I could see how God was using them to recalculate my route. My parents must have been watching too because eventually they saw God's faithfulness and gave their lives to Him as well. What a joyful family reunion awaits us as we all gather in heaven to worship before the throne of our God and King!

In Thought

"Lord, I am so grateful to You that You are my faithful companion as I travel through this life that is filled with unplanned delays, distractions and detours. Through Your Word and Your still, quiet voice You have given me rest along the way and beamed the light of Your love on my path. Thank you for Your company. Amen."

In Word

- *You make known to me the path of life; in your presence there is fullness of joy; at your right hand are pleasures forevermore.* Psalm 16:11 ESV
- *But the path of the righteous is like the light of dawn, which shines brighter and brighter until full day.* Proverbs 4:18 ESV

In Deed

Consider that the trials and detours in life may actually be rest stops along the way, and when you are road-weary, all you need to do is pull into a rest stop and spend a little time with Him.

Janie Southard

89
Don't Sweat
the Small Stuff

The master said, "Well done, my good and faithful
servant. You have been faithful in handling this
small amount, so now I will give you many more
responsibilities. Let's celebrate together!"
Matthew 25:23 NLT

My hand shook so hard the white pills almost fell out of the small little cup. I stopped and took a deep breath to calm my nerves. I looked over to see an encouraging nod from my nursing professor. With a forced smile, I pretended that my heart was not pounding out of control and then I willed my hands to be still. "I can do this," I told myself, as I continued slowly walking toward the patient's room. I paused in the doorway and looked at her chart. As I scanned the approved medications, I quickly rattled off the five rights in administering medication under my breath: "1 – the right patient, 2 – the right time and frequency, 3 – the right dose, 4 – the right route of administration, and 5 – the right drug."

I reached the door, knocked and was told to enter. I slowly approached the patient, all the while mustering up confidence so she could not tell that it was my very first time to give a <u>real</u> medication to a <u>real</u> patient! As a nursing student, I had practiced on my roommate with M&M's, but this was the <u>real</u> thing! I glanced over my shoulder to see the nursing professor in her pressed white lab coat, clipboard and pen in hand. She was ready and waiting to record any errors.

That was the moment time stopped for me. Giving this medication would either be the beginning or the end to my nursing career. I had never failed at anything in my life and I was not going to begin now. I asked to check the patient's arm band which she quickly produced. I explained what the pills were for and all the side effects. I then asked if she had any questions about the medication, and to my great relief she said, "No, but don't I need some water?" I quickly grabbed her cup and poured some water almost knocking it over. She swallowed the medication and went back to watching her television show.

I met my nursing professor in the hallway and triumphantly said, "I did it!" She put her clipboard down and smiled as she replied, "Mikelle, you did a great job in there! Now, I think you are ready to administer something stronger than extra strength Tylenol!"

I have to laugh at myself giving those very first pills! I was so scared that I would fail. And yes, they really were just extra strength Tylenol! But that fear almost paralyzed me. Failure meant repeating a level, or worse.

As Christians, we are not given a spirit of timidity or fear. The victory is already ours if Christ Jesus lives within us as the Holy Spirit. When we let fear hold us captive, we miss the blessings and the power that comes through life lived abundantly in Jesus. The only thing we should fear is God and that is an awesome experience of faith and understanding. So, the next time you find yourself paralyzed in fear, remember that the Holy Spirit that dwells in you is the power of God. Remember you are a victorious child of God and that all things are possible, even giving your first Tylenol to your first patient. Just like the bumper sticker says: "Don't sweat the small stuff…and it's all small stuff!"

In Thought

"Lord, give me a spirit of power, love and self discipline that comes only from you. Remove all fear and darkness from me for You are the light of the world. I want to be a good and faithful servant to You with what gifts and abilities you have given me. Amen."

In Word

For God has not given us a spirit of fear and timidity, but of power, love, and self-discipline. 2 Timothy 1:7 NLT

In Deed

- Make a list of your abilities and gifts and dedicate the list to the Lord to use.
- Remember a time in your life that you experienced great fear of failure. Did you turn to the Lord? Did you overcome that fear or was it victorious over you? Pray today thanking the Lord for helping you overcome fear in the past and any fear that arises in your future.
- Memorize 2 Timothy 1:7 and put it in your memory armor for the next time you experience paralyzing fear.

Mikelle Challenger

90
Let It Shine

You are the light of the world. A city on a hill cannot be hidden. Neither do people light a lamp and put it under a bowl. Instead they put it on its stand, and it gives light to everyone in the house. In the same way, let your light shine before men, that they may see your good deeds and praise your Father in heaven.
Matthew 5:14-16 NIV

The sudden drop in temperature coupled with the howling wind should have been our first clue. But we paid no attention. Lightning flashed silent warnings repeatedly over the horizon, but we headed north anyway. Though we were traveling faster than the brewing storm, we were still along its same path. Nevertheless, we were determined not to let the storm keep us from our weekend retreat.

After an evening of fun, fellowship and worship, we retired to our cabins and drifted peacefully to sleep, still not expecting the storm's wrath to find us. But find us, it did – at 3 a.m. when a sudden clap of thunder jarred us all from sleep. One by one, we climbed out of bed and shuffled around in our socks to peek out of windows and assess the inclement weather. Though some tried to go back to sleep, not one in our cabin of thirty women could find rest with the pounding rain and screaming wind. Rumors of tornadoes circulated and concern for our safety grew. Suddenly, the storm exploded into an abrupt climax of blinding lightning and deafening thunder resulting in the immediate loss of electricity. Our cabin went dark, and it took no time at all for us to realize that not one of us had thought to bring a flashlight.

We stumbled around the unfamiliar surroundings calling out to each other for direction but remaining lost and confused in the darkness. We chided ourselves for not paying attention in Girl Scouts when they lectured us on the necessity of flashlights in the woods and longed for a candle or a match or anything to bring us light.

At last, I had an epiphany. I rummaged under my bunk bed and emerged triumphant with my cell phone. The faint, green glow of the phone was like a beacon of light compared to the black void the storm had caused. We breathed a collective sigh of relief at our unexpected source of light. And though the electricity stayed off for the remainder of the night, we could finally see, for the glow of our digital miracles bathed our surroundings in light and guided our steps.

We live in a dark and fallen world. Like a storm that casts a shadow of darkness along its path, sin covers our eyes and blinds us from the face of God. But if we are in Christ, we have become the light of the world because we have received the source of the light: Jesus.

Sometimes our relationship with Christ is such that our light shines like a spotlight onto the hearts of those around us, but other times, we are less confident in sharing our faith. It helps to remember that even the dimmest of lights, like the faint glow of a cell phone, can provide relief to a world bathed in darkness. We are commanded by Christ to be the light of the world and to share His truth with others, and that command is not dependent upon the strength of our relationship or the brightness of our lights. For our world is so dark and so blind that its eyes ache for a glimmer of light revealing even the slightest glimpse of the Lord. Be that light to someone today.

In Thought

"Dear Lord, thank You that I once was blind but now I see. I know that I am now to be the light of the world, and I pray that You would make me aware of opportunities to share Christ with others. And when those times come, I pray that You would give me the confidence to share my faith boldly. Amen."

In Word

- Your eye is the lamp of your body. When your eyes are good, your whole body also is full of light. But when they are bad, your body also is full of darkness. See to it, then, that the light within you is not darkness. Therefore, if your whole body is full of light, and no part of it dark, it will be completely lighted, as when the light of a lamp shines on you. Luke 11:34-36 NIV
- If I say, "Surely the darkness will hide me and the light become night around me," even the darkness will not be dark to you; the night will shine like the day, for darkness is as light to you. Psalm 139:11-12 NIV
- Let him who walks in the dark, who has no light, trust in the name of the LORD and rely on his God. Isaiah 50:10 NIV

In Deed

- Are you afraid or nervous to share Christ with others? If so, write out your own personal testimony and spend time reflecting on the circumstances and people that led you to the Lord. Doing so will refresh your beliefs and strengthen your confidence.
- Pray for the opportunity to witness to at least one person over the next week. God will be faithful and answer that request. When He does, let your light shine and share the hope that is within you.

Emily Ryan

Week 13 Notes

About the Authors

Dwight Baker is a computer technician by day and freelance writer by night, having written for newspapers, magazines, essay collections, and TV news segments in Houston, Texas. He spent 18 years working at NASA's Johnson Space Center but kept his love for writing to educate and inspire God's people alive in the meantime. Upon leaving NASA he started his own writing business, Lone Star Freelance, and also works for a computer firm in Sugar Land, Texas. He lives with his wife and three children in Pearland, TX.

Cindy Cañas is a stay-at-home mom who dabbles in poetry, Bible study and short autobiographies, and she has been published in "Invoking the Muse." She and her husband, Jason, are the parents of four children, Maddi, Justin, and twins, Jaxson and Jadyn. *Psalm 131*

Mikelle Challenger is a registered nurse who graduated from Azusa Pacific University in Los Angeles, California with a BS in Nursing. She and her husband, Mike, have two young sons, James and Grant. She is now a fulltime stay-at-home mom, which she admits is much more challenging than her nursing career! When she's not writing, she serves as the Ultrasound Sonographer at the Crisis Pregnancy Center of Pasadena.

Patricia Dixon is a native of New Orleans who came to Houston after Hurricane Katrina. She is a retired Occupational Therapist and is a recent graduate from the University of Houston-Clear Lake with her MA in Literature.

Kim Lindquist is a stay-at-home mom to son Garrett and stepmom to adult children Lance and Kristy. She worked for ten years as a technical editor, but writing is her first love! After leading an autism support group for seven years, Kim now works part time for Weight Watchers, advocates for her son, and encourages parents of children with disabilities. She and her husband of 17 years, Mark, love taking trips to the Texas Hill Country with their son, and Kim never tires of traveling with her family! The Lindquist family also attends special events for individuals with disabilities on a regular basis. Kim's latest new love is gardening.

B.J. Massa work in the Missions Ministry at Sagemont Church by day and dabbles in photography and journalism by night. She is married to Joe Massa, and has step-daughters Lauren and Kristin.

Sharon Rigsby is a graduate of the University of Houston with a degree in Business Education and a minor in English. She and her husband, Frank, have a daughter, Gayle, a son, Neil, and three grandchildren. Sharon's passions are photography, painting, gardening, singing in the church choir and traveling on mission trips around the world to tell people about Jesus. Her stories of her mission trip experiences have been published in the magazine *Sagemont Life*.

Emily Ryan is a graduate of Sam Houston State University with an honors degree in English and is the author of *Who Has Your Heart? The Single Woman's Pursuit of Godliness*. In addition to speaking and writing, she works for a financial advisor and serves as Executive Editor for Priority Ministries. She and her husband, Jason, have three children, Gideon, Canaan, and Adelle.

Janie Southard began her writing career at the Houston Chronicle but set it aside over 30 years ago for the blessings of motherhood. Now, with all eight kids fairly self-sufficient, she has once again taken up her pen, or rather, keyboard, to write about the incredible ways God is working in the lives of His people.

Donna Tovander lives with her husband, Lars, in Seabrook, TX, where they assist with photography and journalism. Donna is the author of *Life, Love and Other Stuff*, an anthology containing Christian poetry and stories inspired by her grandparents. She holds a PhD in medicine and in counseling.